Oh My, Au Pair!
A Complete Guide to
Hiring and Hosting an Au Pair

By

Nancy Felix

---

* When calling university,
    start with international studies dept.
    - ask about offerings for J-1 visa
    - check course is offered by
      university faculty
* call CC in Boston, ask to speak w/ travel
* Δ address in account after move...
    will need another site visit

First published by Dog Ear Publishing
4010 W. 86th Street, Ste H
Indianapolis, IN 46268
www.dogearpublishing.net

ISBN: 978-160844-250-8

This book is printed on acid-free paper.

Printed in the United States of America

TABLE OF CONTENTS

INTRODUCTION:

The Speeding Ticket, a Gift to Parents Everywhere

Like most working mothers, I had the morning schedule down to the second. The drop-off routine was a finely choreographed dance. At exactly 7:20 a.m., I would drop off my second-grader, Will, at the elementary school's "before care program." Next, I would drop off four-year-old Hank at day care. I would always be the first to arrive and would kiss Hank on the head before handing him off to a squat Italian woman named Rose at exactly 7:30 a.m., the moment she unlocked the door. I would walk quickly to the car and drive to the train station with no time to stop for coffee. Most days, I would drive into a parking spot, shove quarters into the parking meter, and arrive on the platform just as the train was slowing to a halt, at exactly 7:47 a.m. Once on the train, I would take a deep breath, check my e-mails, and get started on the work that was supposed to have been done the previous day.

It was a precarious existence. There were multiple drop-offs, multiple pickups, and the stress of having to be at the day care by absolutely 5:30 p.m. every day or pay the painful $1-per-minute penalty. Of course, there were also the summer months when school was out and I had to patch together day camps and sitters and family vacations. My husband, Mark, worked in consulting and had a schedule full of business trips and unpredictability. He certainly helped out when he could, but it fell to me (and my 9-to-5 job) to take the lead on child care.

My life was forever changed when New Jersey Transit altered the train schedule. My train now left the station seven minutes earlier, and I clearly did not have an extra seven minutes in my schedule. The next train, a full forty-eight minutes later, would not allow me to work an eight-hour day. I was screwed.

Who would have thought that a train seven minutes earlier would turn my world upside down? But it did. I shaved as much time as I could off the routine. I arrived at day care minutes before they opened. I sprinted to the car. I sped to the station, praying to get every single light green. Some days, I made the train by seconds. Lots of days, I missed it.

About ten days into the new train schedule, I was speeding along the normal route. I looked up, saw flashing lights behind me, and swore. I was driving 50 in a 35 mph zone. That's an expensive and time-consuming ticket! I sat in the driver's seat of the car, watching in my side mirror as the nineteen-year-old patrolman slowly walked up to my car. All I could think of was the conference call that I was surely going to miss.

"Where are you going in such a hurry?" he asked happily. The sun was shining brightly on the wide avenue with perfectly manicured lawns. Why was this young policeman so chipper? I was going to be late!

"The train—it leaves in exactly seven minutes," I stammered, figuring that the faster I spoke, the faster I could talk my way out of a ticket. "New Jersey Transit changed the schedule. The train leaves earlier. It used to be at 7:47. But they changed it to 7:40." I could feel my face getting redder with anxiety, but I continued to plead my case, "But my day care only opens at 7:30 a.m. so I can't drop off my son until then. That only leaves me ten minutes to get to the station. So I have to rush. I have to rush to catch the train."

He clearly did not understand my predicament. "You should give yourself more time," he said with a very serious look on his face.

"I can't! Don't you see? I have to be on that train. The next one is too late!" I yelped. Then I burst out crying, sobbing over my steering wheel. That was it. I was done. I watched him walk back to his car. Very slowly.

I thought, *Please give me a warning. Please do not write me a ticket. That will take forever, and I might even miss the next train!*

He sat in his patrol car for what felt like forever. I watched 7:40 come and go on the clock; that train was gone. The next one was 8:28. Maybe I could still make that. If only he would hurry up! Some time later, the policeman ambled back to the car, ticket in hand. He reduced the speed down to 39 in a 35 so I would not get any points on my license. I suppose I should have been grateful. Really, I was just tired, physically and emotionally exhausted from this stress that I put myself through every weekday. I knew right then I could not sustain it.

The Plight of the Working Mom

At some point, most working mothers experience some kind of event that serves as a catalyst to change. For some mothers, it's the sixth or seventh ear infection that ruins a good night's sleep or a nanny who just doesn't show up for work one morning. For me, it was that speeding ticket.

Some working mothers cash it in and decide to stay at home. Others change jobs or careers to find a work environment that is more flexible. I knew that something had to change, but I did not want to stop working.

I am not a high-powered mom with a jet-setting job. My children go to public schools, and my dining room table is cluttered with coupons and catalogues. I am a commuter: one who shops online for overstocks and does the grocery shopping at 9:00 at night. From my desk in New York City, I make doctor appointments, and, whenever I can, sneak out of work early so my boys have their mom with them at the orthodontist or pediatrician. I read to Will and Hank at night and take them to birthday parties where I know few other parents. I manage the finances of our house and the day-to-day routines. I struggle to find time to exercise and wish I could lose a few pounds.

I admit that I am a working mom who is content sending in Whole Foods brownies for the bake sale (the "Two Bite Brownies" are my favorite). I am perfectly happy having someone else pick up my kids from school. I'm very comfortable volunteering at school two or three times per year and not having to be the class mom. I am secure in my working motherhood. In fact, I really like it. I value earning my own money and enjoy reading books on the train. I thrive on the intellectual stimulation and the opportunity to contribute in a team environment. And I'll be honest: I *love* the occasional business trip when I can have a hotel-room bed all to myself.

When I got that speeding ticket, I was forced to admit that my childcare arrangements simply did not work. Juggling the day care, after care, before care, summer camp, and vacation schedules was getting really complicated (not to mention stressful). But I knew that I could do it. As a teenager, I had mastered the schoolwork while participating on the varsity field hockey team and singing in the a cappella group. I had always been able to balance the different parts of my life. So as a working mom, I knew that I could do it. I just needed to get the childcare piece right.

That speeding ticket brought it all to a head. My husband, Mark, and I talked. He knew how much I love being a mom and how much I love working. We decided that it was time to try a new solution. We decided to hire an au pair.

Hiring and Hosting an Au Pair

I did my research—to the extent possible. But I soon learned that there was no one who could offer me objective advice and give me the straight scoop.

I contacted several au pair agencies who put me in touch with their local coordinators in my area. From the local coordinators, I learned about the benefits of having an au pair. I learned how many other au pairs were living in my town. I was informed of the basic requirements to be a host family.

I spoke to other host families. Though not the most objective resources, my host mother friends confirmed that the au pair program is convenient and cost effective. I heard about an au pair who totaled the family car during her first week. One family loved Brazilian girls who were "affectionate" and "loving." Another only hired German girls who were "reliable" and "organized." One family insisted that their au pair always go on family vacations. Another was thrilled that their au pair traveled with her boyfriend every weekend. There was little consensus, except that all the host families shared a desire to have their children grow up with a global perspective.

I read articles and learned that the au pair program has really changed in recent years. Both convenient and affordable, it is the fastest-growing segment of the childcare market. In 2008, 22,000 young women and men came to the United States to care for children in exchange for an inside look at American culture. I learned that an au pair is not a nanny and that the terms should not be interchanged.

I was sure that we would be the perfect host family, just because we are such normal people. But that was eight years ago, before I understood the complexities of host parenting and being an au pair. I have learned a lot in eight years. I have had fourteen au pairs, and each has taught me something worth holding onto. They came from countries all over the world with wildly different backgrounds. My boys like to remind me that we have had au pairs from every continent, except Antarctica. (When and if an au pair from Antarctica ever applies to the program, she's mine!) Each decided to be an au pair for a different reason, and each grew tremendously from the experience. A few au pairs were fabulous. A few were just OK. Only one was truly awful.

The good news is that my kids are not scarred for life. In fact, I think they consider the world a smaller place than do their peers. They look at getting a new au pair the same way they look at getting a new classroom teacher each September. Because we have had au pairs, Will and Hank are open to people who look different and sound different. They even know a few words of Japanese, German, and Afrikaans. I am hoping that this might help on their college applications some day.

I am the one who has been most changed by the experience. Having all these au pairs has made me a better mom.

When I picked up our first au pair, a smart Slovakian girl named Vera, I was a rookie. I didn't know a thing. Sure, I had read the materials from the au pair agency and listened intently to the advice of the local coordinator, but I still made many mistakes.

What I really needed was a manual.

Eight years, fourteen au pairs, and one speeding ticket later, I have gained significant insight and experience and have brought it all together in *Oh My, Au Pair! A Complete Guide to Hiring and Hosting an Au Pair*. In these pages, I share the specifics of the program and reveal the secrets to choosing an au pair who is compatible with your family. You will learn how to optimize the experience for your au pair and your family. I'll provide advice for incorporating him or her into your family. You will learn about what happens when things go wrong with your au pair. You will also see why having an au pair enriches the lives of your children and your family in a way no other childcare arrangement ever could.

The vast majority of au pairs in the United States are female. Most au pair agencies don't even recruit male au pairs. So throughout this book, I will refer to au pairs by using the feminine pronoun. This is for convenience only. I mean no offense to the male au pairs who read this book. Nor am I advocating female au pairs over male au pairs. With a fourteen-year-old boy in my house now (who is taller and stronger than me), I will likely go back to having a male au pair the next time around … whenever that will be.

Meet My Au Pairs

My fourteen au pairs have helped make this how-to guide happen. I am grateful that they have allowed me to share our experiences, but I have changed their names to respect their privacy. Because so many of their stories fill this book, allow me to briefly introduce you to each of them.

Au Pair #1: Vera
Vera was a twenty-four-year-old Eastern European seamstress who came to America with a secret plan. When she arrived, her English was terrible, and we spent the first several months muddling through misunderstandings. We carefully circled one another and never connected. Vera always looked unhappy, and I couldn't do anything to help, until she found a boyfriend at the local rock-climbing gym. Then she disappeared and hatched a secret plan to stay in the United States. It was my first au pair experience, and I was learning the ropes. Vera was as smart as a whip but only a fair au pair. After her year with us, she stayed in America, went to university, graduated cum laude, and is now quite a success story, thanks in part to my father, who helped her to get into college and file her visa paperwork.

Au Pair #2: Kit
After Vera, we wanted someone who spoke English well and would play with the kids. We chose Kit from New Zealand. The youngest of four girls from a sheep-farming family on the South Island, this Kiwi was a big eighteen-year-old and worked in the small-town delicatessen. She was happy-go-lucky and a terrible housekeeper. She was with us for eleven months. On the phone, Kit was goofy and giggly. We thought she was funny and loved her accent. She was sweet and had great aspirations for her "gap year." A "gap year" is very

much a part of the culture in New Zealand and Australia; it is a time for young people to travel the world for a year or so before settling down to working or going to university. Kit had recently finished high school and was ready to see the world and eager to experience America. She loved the children, and we were glad she spoke English.

Au Pair #3: Andrea
Our third au pair was our first rematch. Arriving in the dead of winter, Andrea suffered extreme culture shock. After Kit, we had thought we needed someone a bit more mature. A tall, professional young woman from Brazil, Andrea seemed ambitious and well-educated. She liked dancing salsa and samba. She told me about the condo at the beach that she had purchased with her older sister and described (in very good English) trips that she would take on the weekends. She owned a car and drove all over Brazil for her job in the insurance field. She loved spending time with her mother and father and three sisters. On paper, Andrea was an accomplished young woman. She had graduated from university with a degree, specializing in international business, but the prospects for job advancement in Brazil were dismal. If she came to America, she could improve her English and thus be better qualified for employment back home. But Andrea was a girlie-girl and not compatible with my active boys. After three months of Andrea being freezing cold and my boys being miserable, we rematched, and Andrea went to live happily with another family.

Au Pair #4: KiKi
KiKi from Japan was our fourth au pair, and we finally knew what a great cultural exchange the au pair program could provide. A Lucy Liu look-alike, KiKi was not an average Japanese woman. She sparkled. KiKi's family was huge by

Japanese standards, with four children (two boys and two girls), KiKi being the oldest. Her father was a working fine artist, a pottery sculptor who made delicate and beautiful porcelains. They had a studio and a home on several acres of land in the countryside near Nagasaki. According to KiKi, the decision to come to America had pretty much assured her that she would never be fully welcomed back to Japanese society. That was just fine with her. Like Vera, KiKi had come to America with a specific plan of what she wanted to accomplish. But unlike Vera, KiKi was up-front and honest about what she wanted to do. Using the au pair educational requirement, she immersed herself in the New York City fashion industry and made friends and contacts. KiKi taught my boys some Japanese and how to make sushi. We had regular houseguests from Japan, and she incubated a small fashion business. She wore pointy shoes, funky hats, and glittery eye makeup. KiKi was a great au pair.

Au Pair #5: Bobby
Before she left, KiKi helped us choose our fifth au pair: Bobby, a twenty-one-year-old very tall guy from Germany. Bobby had completed "gymnasium," the German equivalent of college preparatory high school, but had not gotten into the university he wanted, so he had decided to come to the U.S. to improve his English and experience America. Eventually, he wanted to study graphic design. He was really good with computers and rode a motocross bike. Bobby had a little sister who had a disability, and he had often been in charge of her care while his parents worked. Bobby was really tall and really thin, with short blonde hair, a chiseled jaw, and bright blue eyes (think Justin Timberlake plus ten inches). Even though Bobby wasn't all that easy to get to know, he wasn't hard to live with, either. He was reliable, meticulous, and thorough. His English was good, and he was great with the boys. While our au pair, Bobby had a hobby that quickly became a profession and then blossomed

into a career. In New York City, Bobby was discovered as a male model. His career took off, and Bobby moved to Milan after only six months in the States. We rematched again.

Au Pair #6: Lena
After Bobby's sudden departure, we didn't have much of a choice in the pool of applicants. We knew we wanted someone over twenty-one with childcare experience and chose our sixth au pair, Lena, based on those requirements. She was our first real mismatch. On paper, Lena from the Czech Republic looked almost perfect. She was twenty-six years old and had one younger brother. She played ice hockey and soccer and loved to go to the movies. Best of all, she had been an au pair in England for two years for a family with two boys, one of whom was autistic. Aside from a professed Madonna obsession and being the only child of a divorced mom, Lena seemed like a perfect match for our family. But it was not perfect. Within days of her arrival, she revealed a drinking problem and a tendency for temper tantrums. After two agonizing months of her partying and bizarre outbursts, we rematched again. Lena was out.

Au Pair #7: Helen
On the phone, Helen sounded like she was from Milwaukee, Wisconsin, not Bergen, Norway. Her English was perfect. She was nineteen years old and highly educated, the eldest daughter of two university professors. Her father was a noted Norwegian economist. Her mother was a professor of psychology who trained astronauts how to cope in space. Helen was serious about her schooling and wanted to take competitive college courses. She read college textbooks in her spare time. Before buckling down to a life in academia, Helen wanted to be an au pair and experience another culture. Unfortunately, Helen arrived at our house one very sick girl.

She had an eating disorder, and despite all our efforts to get her help here in America, she and her family decided that she had to go home for treatment. We rematched again.

Au Pair #8: Sally

Sally, from Germany, restored my sanity. At twenty-three, Sally was mature, very tall, and blonde, with olive skin and green, droopy eyes. Sally had been born in the Netherlands but moved to Bavaria, Germany, when she was ten. She was laid-back, liked to drink beer, and was very even-tempered. She had a comforting calm about her that inspired confidence. After Helen, Sally was a breeze. She loved our dog and was easy to live with. Sally stayed almost a year. We begged her to extend her stay for another year, but she had to return to Germany to work in her family's business.

Au Pair #9: Carla

Our ninth au pair was Jin Hee, code name Carla. It is a custom in Korea for people to adopt English names, and most of these new names have absolutely no relation to their given names. During the phone interview, Carla was deliberate with her words but gave good reasons for wanting to come to America. She had completed university with a degree in English literature. She loved Jane Austen and Hemingway. She had a boyfriend who was beginning his two-year obligatory military service. Her mother was a massage therapist, and her father worked on a mandarin orange farm. Carla had three sisters; she was the second of the four. Her older sister was a waitress in a restaurant, and her younger sisters were still in school. She lived on an island off the coast of Korea that looked a great deal like Hawaii with beaches, a volcano, and palm trees. Carla seemed sweet. But once she arrived, we knew almost immediately it was a disaster. There was a profound communication barrier. The match lasted two months.

Au Pair #10: Karen

After Carla, we hit the au pair jackpot. Our tenth au pair was Karen. This petite Angelina Jolie look-alike was from South Africa. She loved New York City and had a fabulous American boyfriend. She considered herself social, independent, positive, and active. She spent hours reading books while curled up on the couch with our dog at her feet but went religiously to the gym every day. She was stunningly beautiful, and she loved my boys. Her English was flawless. She was with us for seven perfect months. Then, her father was killed in a boating accident in a gaming preserve in South Africa. Karen, along with her boyfriend, Brian, returned to Africa and began the rest of their lives together.

Au Pair #11: Sabrina

This time, we chose Sabrina from Germany, a sweet girl who was half Thai and half German. At her home in Hamburg, she worked three jobs, and her English was great. She seemed excited for an adventure. Unfortunately for us, she had fallen in love with a German boy three weeks before coming to America. She spent hours on the phone, on the computer, and sending packages to her new boyfriend. She never got over her homesickness, and after four months, she couldn't take it anymore. Sabrina bailed.

Au Pair #12: Elisa

Sabrina did give us a little notice, and I spent several weeks interviewing au pairs before offering the job to Elisa from Sweden. Elisa made friends quickly; she was good with the kids; and she was easy to live with. Her group of Swedish au pairs spent weekends with the local soccer coaches who were also in the States on J-1 visas. Several romances emerged. Elisa's family came for a visit and introduced us to the Swedish lawn game Kub. We had a great year with Elisa.

Au Pair #13: Marta
Next, I hired a nice girl from Germany. Marta was the youngest of four kids. Two of her older siblings were au pairs, so I figured that she would really know what she was getting herself into. She did. She immediately connected with the boys and played hours of Monopoly. She was a great driver and quickly learned the easiest route to the rock-climbing gym. From the first day, I never stressed. The boys really liked Marta. Unfortunately, she arrived during the so-called swine flu epidemic. When my youngest came down with a cough and a low-grade fever, Marta freaked out. Her parents demanded that she return home. At the age of nineteen and still very much in the family fold, Marta caved to her family's demand. She left abruptly on a Saturday morning, barely saying good-bye.

Au Pair #14: Nina
Our fourteenth au pair is Nina, from South Africa. She arrived a few weeks ago and is getting to know my kids and learning the ropes. I am crossing my fingers!

CHAPTER 1:

IT'S A CULTURAL-EXCHANGE PROGRAM

The French phrase *au pair* translates loosely to "as an equal." Theoretically, an au pair is someone living with you "on your par." In exchange for forty-five hours of childcare per week, a host family provides an au pair with the experience of living in America and learning about a new culture—a cultural exchange. The au pair relationship is supposed to be for one year, though it can be extended for a second year. Begun by the United States Department of State in 1986 with only three hundred au pairs, the au pair movement has seen a dramatic expansion in recent years. There are now approximately twenty thousand au pairs in the United States in any one year, and the program continues to grow rapidly. The agency I use "imported" almost five thousand au pairs to the States in 2008 alone.

My family bears some responsibility for this increase.

An Au Pair Is Not a Nanny

When I got that speeding ticket and realized I could not continue the day care, before care, after care childcare arrangement, I first looked into having a regular nanny. This was how many of my commuting friends handled their childcare needs. They would call up a nanny agency, pay a nominal fee, and interview several nanny candidates from Trinidad, Jamaica, Brazil, Russia, or the Ukraine, and in a day or so, they would have a live-in or live-out nanny. A live-out is someone who would come to their house every morning, watch the kids, and ferry the kids to and from school, playdates, lessons, and practices. The nanny would do the grocery shopping, do the laundry, iron, and even clean the house. A live-in does all these things and lives in the home.

I talked to several moms I knew from commuting who employed nannies. Their experiences made me question if it was the right solution for me. I heard good stories and bad stories. One friend had had a live-out nanny for four years, starting right after their first son was born. The nanny was great with the baby, did laundry, kept the house clean, and was trustworthy and reliable. She was a lovely woman who genuinely loved their child. But the costs seemed really high. She started at a salary of $500 per week and every few months, predictably asked for a raise. Within a year, they had increased her salary to $575 per week, which came out to about $30,000 per year. With all this paid after taxes, I figured that close to $60,000 of my salary would be needed just to cover the child care. I just didn't earn the kind of money that exceeds the economic break-even point for employing a nanny.

TIP: With an au pair, you never have to get a weekend babysitter. Schedule your "date night" into her regular working hours.

Economics aside, there were some stories that scared me. My friend Paula had a live-in nanny, Sandra, who stayed with them during the week but then went home on the weekend. One Monday morning, Sandra hadn't shown up for work. And Paula was missing a credit card. She had torn the house apart, and when she couldn't find it, she had called the bank to report it stolen. The last charge had been an $800 payment made to a dress salon in New Jersey called Wedding Belles. Sandra had eloped, and Paula had paid for the wedding dress. She had been a victim of fraud, not to mention that she had been left in the lurch, without child care.

Let's face it: Most live-in and live-out nannies are in this country illegally, which means that they have no health insurance and little to no savings. One family had a nanny for two years and called her Monique, only to find out that Monique's real name was Maria and she had used another person's identity to get in the country, establish herself, and get a job.

Of course, there are many wonderful nannies out there. But there are inherent limitations with the live-in or live-out nanny. Live-out nannies are usually older and may prefer certain age ranges of children. They may have children of their own that they are also looking after. Nannies will likely do more around your house – clean, grocery shop, and run errands. The cost is significantly higher than having an au pair, and a live-out nanny may have to be home at the same time everyday. Live-out nannies are usually not very flexible when you have to work late or go in to the office early. I had a somewhat regular work schedule, but every once in a while, I would go through a rough patch, with early-morning breakfast meetings and evening events, so I needed to know that there would be flexibility at home.

With an au pair, the pay is set, the hours are set, and the job duties are set out in the very beginning. Almost all details of the au pair– host family relationship are regulated by the State Department. There is little to negotiate. There are higher authorities to consult and advise. I like that sort of backup.

I just don't have the backbone for a nanny. A goody two-shoes to the core, I live on the straight and narrow, never willing to break any law (except speeding). I'm not good at firing an employee. I have never been good at saying "no" to people. I always look for the good in people and can be gullible. If I had a nanny, I am afraid she would walk all over me. If

17

she asked for a raise, I would give it to her and then stew about it for weeks, resenting her power over me.

The J-1 Visa

The au pair program is technically a cultural-exchange program. Au pairs come to the United States on a J-1 visa. Administered by the U.S. Department of State, the J-1 visa allows people from foreign countries to temporarily work in the United States. This is the same category of visa that allows foreign professors to teach at American universities. It is the same visa that allows for foreign summer-camp counselors and seasonal-resort employees. Though the au pair program is a small category within the larger "guest worker" exchange program, it is big business.

The J-1 visa is valid for twelve months, though an au pair can now extend the visa for an additional six, nine, or twelve months. This new option has greatly improved the attractiveness of the program and is somewhat responsible for how much the program has grown lately. If all goes well, an au pair can be with you for two years. I have never been that lucky.

In exchange for forty-five hours of child care, an American host family provides the young person with an experience living in the United States and a stipend of $175 per week. The program is heavily regulated by the State Department, and there are only a dozen officially sanctioned agencies that legally place au pairs with American families. In addition to sharing our culture, part of our responsibility as a host family is to provide the au pair with a $500 educational stipend to earn six credits or take at least sixty hours of classes at a local university.

Who Can Be an Au Pair? And Why Would They Want to?

A young person who chooses to come to America and work as an au pair knows that she is coming to the United States for a "cultural exchange," not a high-paying job. An au pair is not in it for the money.

There are very few qualifying prerequisites for an au pair to apply to the program. At a minimum, a young person must

✓ Have previous childcare experience.

✓ Be between the ages of eighteen and twenty-six.

✓ Be a high school graduate (called "secondary school" in the rest of the world).

✓ Be proficient in spoken English (using a very loose definition of "proficient").

✓ Have no criminal record.

✓ Be in good health.

✓ Be able to commit to a twelve-month position.

An au pair must also get an International Driving Permit and have fifty hours of driving experience.

Obviously, each and every au pair has a different reason for choosing to spend a year or so taking care of someone else's children in America. In my experience, they fit into one of two categories: the "gap-year" au pairs or the "great-escape" au pairs.

The "Gap-Year" Au Pairs
These au pairs have something real and serious to go back to in their home countries, and they are using the au pair

experience as a way of postponing the inevitable, whether that be university or a real job. I've found that au pairs from the Scandinavian and European countries usually fit into this category. They are usually eighteen or nineteen years old and come to America with a shopping list and an itinerary of travel destinations. They make friends quickly. Their English is great. They don't care if they bring home even one dollar (especially because the dollar isn't worth much in their home countries), so they spend every dollar they make. There is very little chance that a gap-year au pair is going to extend and stay a second year with you.

Our eighth au pair, Sally, is a perfect example of the gap-year au pair. She came to the United States to be an au pair, knowing that she had a job in her family business waiting for her. Her family had obliged her wish to take a year off, and she took advantage of everything in the U.S. She traveled, made great friends, and did a lot of shopping. But when it came time to go home, she was resolute. She had an obligation and had spent her time playing. She was ready to really get to work.

The "Great Escape" Au Pairs
These au pairs have big plans. They come here because the opportunities in their home countries are so limited that if they want to succeed, they must escape their current situations. They come here to learn English, make as much money as possible, and, with any luck, figure out a way to stay in the States after the au pair program has ended. I've found that these au pairs are usually from Eastern European countries, South American countries, or Thailand. Some send money home to their families. Others save like crazy to support their post-au pair days. Great-escape au pairs are more likely to stay a second year so they can save more money and further

their plans to stay in the United States. The great-escape au pairs are believers in the American dream, and being an au pair is their first step toward realizing that dream.

Our first au pair, Vera, is a perfect example of this type of au pair. She spent the entire year with us, planning how to stay in the United States. After her au pair year, she transferred her J-1 visa to a "student visa" (which is an F-1 or M-1 visa). She stayed in the country legally and completed her studies while working for several different families. She graduated from university, got a job, and was married to her boyfriend. She is now a tax-paying, productive member of society, living the American dream.

Some great-escape au pairs don't play by the rules. Justine was an au pair in our town from Poland. Her English was very difficult to understand, making conversation very challenging. She was absolutely obsessed with herself and worked very hard to be attractive. She would spend hours getting ready in the morning, applying her makeup, doing her hair, making sure her outfit was perfectly coordinated. And what was she getting ready for? Schlepping the kids to and from school, helping with homework, making dinner, and doing laundry. But she always wanted to be ready for her close-up. She had come to America to be "discovered," and she was sure that someone who saw her at the school playground or at the grocery store or in the coffee shop downtown would swoop in and pluck her away to a life of glamour, fortune, and fame.

She once wore a gold lamé evening gown to babysit the kids while the host parents were having a dinner party. She wore hot pants and platform heels to baseball games (she did have nice legs). To soccer practice, she wore pancake makeup and was sure to have a matching handbag to her outfit. She would stay out late, smoke in the house when the parents were out, and never let her host family know where she was going. During the day, she snuck off to NYC, where she was "auditioning" for "movies." She lasted through the year, but the family was not happy. And when the day finally came for her to leave, she was picked up by "a friend" and just disappeared. She did not even bother to take with her the return plane ticket to Poland. Gone. Poof. Into thin air. Into the au pair underground. The family worries that she is now a porn star, or worse.

The Louise Woodward Legacy

Remember Louise Woodward? Many years ago, she was the au pair who gave the whole au pair program a really bad name and a serious shakeup.

Louise was a young woman from England who was hired as an au pair to care for an eight-month-old boy, Matthew Eapen, near Boston, Massachusetts. Louise came to America as an au pair when she was eighteen. She had little childcare experience, especially with infants. She worked long hours and did not have many friends. She was isolated and lonely.

I really don't know what happened in that house the day that the baby boy died. Some experts called it shaken baby syndrome. Others disagreed. But there is no denying that Matthew's death was a huge tragedy and should not have happened. Louise was convicted of involuntary manslaughter, sentenced to time served, and now lives in England. Since this happened in 1997, the au pair program has changed significantly.

The au pair program as we know it today is shaped largely by the Louise Woodward incident. The regulations, guidelines, and standards mandated by the State Department changed drastically after the incident—to protect both host families and their au pairs. The strict rules now in place and the mandatory support networks are designed to prevent this sort of horror story from ever happening again.

Under the stricter rules, all au pairs must go through an orientation upon their arrival in the States. They must also have background checks and face-to-face screenings in their home countries. As a veteran au pair host mom, I really don't think that these two things alone will prevent another tragedy from happening. The best change was the addition of the local coordinator and the mandated "cluster" activities. Having the coordinator (who is also a counselor, mediator, and troubleshooter) and other au pairs nearby creates a needed support network for au pairs who might be feeling lonely or stressed out. This is a good thing.

The Role of the Coordinator

The official regulations from the State Department (post Louise Woodward) require each agency to have a local representative who lives no more than fifty miles from your home. The coordinator is in charge of a "cluster" of au pairs and their host families; usually about fifty families are in a cluster. The tasks of the coordinator are incredibly varied.

The coordinator organizes monthly activities, known as "cluster events," for the au pairs. The cluster events are quasi-mandatory for the au pairs. The events encourage the au pairs to socialize and get to know one another. The result is a built-in support network that the au pairs need, so that when they are feeling lonely, homesick, or stressed out, they have someone to turn to for help.

In our cluster, the coordinator has organized events such as bowling, painting pottery, white-water rafting, snow tubing, ice skating in Central Park, nights at the movies, going to Yankees games, and get-togethers at a local coffee house on an open-mic night. I wish she would organize my social life. I might see my friends more often.

The coordinator helps new au pairs transition into their cultural exchange by introducing au pairs to one another and circulating lists of au pairs whenever new au pairs join the cluster. She e-mails the au pairs constantly, reminding them who is new, who is having a birthday, and who is leaving soon. She encourages new au pairs to get out, and she encourages old au pairs to reach out to the new ones. She is like the au pair den mother.

The coordinator also markets the program to new families. She interviews prospective host families in their homes and conducts a "site visit" to make sure that they can and will fulfill the requirements of being a host family. She makes sure that there is a separate bedroom for the au pair.

After the au pair's arrival, the coordinator will come to the house for an orientation, where she has the family and the new au pair sign a "childcare contract" in which each pledges to play by the rules. At the orientation, the local coordinator gets first impressions and begins to monitor the relationship.

After the in-home orientation, the coordinator is required by the agency to do monthly check-ins by telephone with all her host families and au pairs. An e-mail to the coordinator does not count; she must speak to the host parent by telephone. When she gets a bad report, she goes into mediation mode. This is the single most important thing that the coordinator does—helping host families when things aren't going well. She counsels the au pairs if they are homesick, having trouble with the children, or don't like the host parents. She counsels the host parents if the au pair is not living up to expectations. She comes to your house, sits in your living room, and serves as the peacemaker, counselor, and consoler. If the match is bad, you will become good friends with the coordinator.

TIP: When the coordinator calls for the monthly check-in, call her back. If things are going well, the call will take thirty seconds. If things are not going well, you might just need a shoulder to cry on.

The coordinator for our cluster is a dead-ringer for Halle Berry. She is petite, stylish, efficient, full of energy, and a straight shooter. She is a cruise director, a therapist, a mediator, and a sales rep. As a day job, she acts in commercials and sings in a gospel choir. She takes no crap from "the girls."

Local coordinators are compensated by the agencies by the number of families in a cluster. If your cluster has fifty families (the average cluster size), the coordinator is making one hundred calls per month—fifty to the au pair and fifty to the host parents. This is no easy job.

The Economics of Having an Au Pair

Assuming your kids are school-age, an au pair is a great and inexpensive childcare option. I have done the math, and the total cost to our family is about $18,000 per year. Let's break down the costs.

You pay the agency a big, whopping fee up front. This usually is between $6,000 and $7,000, depending on which agency you use. This fee covers transportation for your au pair to your town (or at least the nearest major airport), Au Pair Academy (a three-day training program after her arrival in the States), health insurance for your au pair, and the mediation and conflict-resolution services of the coordinator (priceless!). The agency has to make money, too. It is, after all, a business.

There is discussion among host parents and some legislators that this fee arrangement is not in the best interest of the customers. Once the agency has your fee, there is little incentive to provide ongoing support or customer service. Reform, in the form of a pay-as-you-go monthly fee arrangement to the agencies, is the answer, many think, because it would force agencies to provide the customer service that would prevent many rematches.

You then pay the au pair $195.75 per week, which comes out to $10,179 per year. In our house, our au pair contributes $5 per week toward her membership at the local YMCA. Some families pick up the whole tab for the gym membership, but I figure if she is paying for it a bit, she will use it. The YMCA is a great place for her to make friends, keep busy, and work off the potato bread and Oreos that she is eating.

You do not have to withhold taxes for your au pair, but you do get to claim the agency fee on your taxes. The au pair is responsible for filing her own tax return and for paying the few hundred dollars that she will owe in income taxes.

TIP: Partially pay for the membership at a local gym and ask your coordinator what gym the au pairs join. This is a great way for your au pair to make friends and keep off the "au pair fifteen."

In addition, you must contribute $500 toward the au pair's educational requirement (more about that later). Incidental costs include an increase in your car insurance and a larger grocery bill every week. After all, there is another mouth to feed.

Finally, you should budget in a few hundred dollars for the "damage deposit." There might be the occasional scrape to the car, the overflowing bathtub that leaked to the room below, the lost beach towels, or the odd broken dishes. With another family member living in your house, stuff happens!

So the grand total includes your fee to the agency, the au pair's weekly stipends, the educational requirement, and other incidental costs, and comes to (in round numbers) about $17,000–$19,000 per year. This is a far cry from the $30,000–$50,000 you might pay for a nanny. Plus, it is all legal, so you can still run for office someday.

The Oligopoly of Agencies

Exactly twelve agencies are licensed by the State Department to recruit and place au pairs. In government lingo, these agencies are called "sponsoring organizations." We have stuck with our agency because their online matching system is great and I love our local coordinator (but more about her in a minute). What you really need to know is that the agencies all offer the same basic services because these services are mandated by the State Department. The result of this oligopoly is that there are only two real differences that you need to be aware of among the agencies.

First, each agency has recruiting partners in different countries around the world. So if you really want an au pair from a certain country or an au pair who speaks a certain language, you should find out which agencies recruit from which countries. To do that, you can visit the Web sites and read up on each agency, or call them and ask.

Second, each agency has a local coordinator who will be your advocate and friend. You should meet the local coordinators for the agencies that serve your area. This relationship must be a good match, because if things go bad with your au pair, the local coordinator will step in for mediation. If you live in a remote or rural location, you may be out of luck. The au pair regulations require that a host family live within fifty miles of a local coordinator. You will need to check with each agency to see if they have a local coordinator in your area.

Somehow, au pairs find each other and become friends, regardless of their agencies. So do not be concerned if your agency has fewer au pairs in your town than another. You should make your decision about the agency based on the two aforementioned factors: recruiting partners and the local coordinator.

For the record, here's the list of the anointed twelve sponsoring agencies:

1. Agent Au Pair (www.agentaupair.com)

2. American Cultural Exchange (www.goAuPair)

3. American Institute for Foreign Study
   (www.aupairinamerica.com)

4. Au Pair Foundation, Inc.
   (www.aupairfoundation.org)

5. Au Pair International, Inc. (www.aupairint.com)

6. AuPairCare, Inc. (www.aupaircare.com)

7. Cultural Care, Inc. (www.culturalcare.com)

8. Cultural Homestay International
   (www.chiaupairusa.org)

9. Euraupair Intercultural Child Care Programs
   (www.euraupair.com)

10. Expert Group International, Inc.
    (www.expertaupair.com)

11. InterExchange Au Pair (www.aupairusa.org)

12. USAuPair, Inc. (www.USAupair.com)

The au pair agencies are big business, and they are growing fast. Across the country, area coordinators market the program to new families and provide some support to au pairs and host families. Like most businesses, more host families mean more profit for the au pair agency. Their economic imperative is to get as many families as they can in the program. Making sure those families are ready, willing, and able to be good host parents is not exactly the agency's highest priority. Sure, they provide some training to the au pairs. But as a host family, you are pretty much on your own to figure out "host parenting" as you go.

The *Wall Street Journal* Told Me I Could Do It

So you may be asking yourself the question, "Is the au pair program right for my family and me?" I asked myself the same question shortly after getting that speeding ticket. To find the answer, I looked where I look for advice on just about everything: the *Wall Street Journal*. In an article on parenting and family matters, there was an analysis of the pros and cons of having an au pair. Here is their "Au Pair Checklist" and my response from eight years ago.

"This childcare option works for some families, not all. Choose an au pair only if you:

> *"... can limit her work to forty-five hours a week, ten hours a day."*

I ran the numbers. On average, our au pair would work about twenty-five hours: five hours a day during the workweek— two hours in the morning and then about three hours in the afternoon doing the after-school shift with the kids. And there might be some weeks that are actually thirty hours because there are some mornings that I have to go in early or stay late. So a forty-five-hour workweek was totally and completely reasonable. In fact, I could build in weekend babysitting hours and ensure the regular date night with my husband.

> *"... have a private bedroom available."*

Check! Built in 1890, our house is a big farmhouse Victorian with a covered porch that wraps around the house from the front door to the back door. There are five bedrooms and three full baths. The third floor of our house has two bedrooms and a private bathroom—a perfect au pair suite.

"… value cross-cultural experiences."

Sure! We liked the idea that our kids would get to know people from other cultures and learn that the world is a big place and we are not the center of it. Mark and his family lived in Austria for five years while he was growing up. My sister lives in Spain. Knowing that the chances of us living abroad were unlikely, the idea of learning about a new culture appealed to me. Besides, the kids might learn some new languages along the way.

"… can care for the emotions of a teen or young adult."

OK! I had been a nanny for two summers when I was a teenager. Having been through a similar experience, I was sure that I could relate to the emotional aspects of being an au pair. At the ages of fifteen and sixteen, I worked seven days a week with babies and young children. I did laundry and changed diapers. I made beets in a pressure cooker and prepared tomato-and-mayonnaise sandwiches. I taught kids to swim and play tennis. I wiped bottoms and did loads and loads of laundry. At times, I was lonely, but I took up running and started field hockey season in the best shape of my life. With these experiences as background, I was sure that I could be a good host mom. I would be sensitive to homesickness, encourage our au pair to get out and meet friends, and make sure that she had time off to pursue her own interests.

"… can help and train an inexperienced caregiver."

Yes! In fact, we had briefly had a live-in babysitter before who had needed help and training. For the two previous summers, we had employed a fabulous young woman from Kansas State University to be our summer babysitter. Bonnie was a farm girl from rural Kansas who was smart, hardworking, and loving. She was pre-med in college, responsible, pleasant, and athletic. She was pretty much perfect. But she had never been a nanny before and had needed help in learning to drive on crowded roads, navigate public transportation, and manage the day-to-day of the kids. It had worked out wonderfully because she was open to learning new things. Bonnie had set the bar.

"... will treat her like a member of the family."

Of course we would! Some people just cannot have a stranger living in their house. We don't mind. We have nothing to hide. No dirty secrets lurking here. We don't bicker or fight. Neither Mark nor I have a temper. We are not prone to walking around in our underwear. We don't smoke. I don't think we have any bizarre habits, besides watching every single televised Yankees baseball game. We don't have any strange exotic pets like snakes or spiders. We are from fun-loving families that play games after dinner and like having friends and family over. This would be an easy one. Our experience with Bonnie showed us that we could have a young person live with us and treat her like a member of the family. We saw how much the boys had grown to love her and truly valued the relationship that she had built with them. We would definitely treat our au pair like a member of the family.

"... don't mind changing caregivers after two years— or sooner."

Not at all! In the beginning, we didn't think twice about this. There was always change in our house. We traveled a lot and always had friends and family visiting. Actually, we thought that change would be good for our boys, by exposing them to several different cultures. Little did we know how much change they would experience: fourteen au pairs in eight years.

So the *Wall Street Journal* gave me confidence that I could be a good host mom. I then looked for the real requirements, the ones from the au pair agencies. To participate in the program as a host family, you must

✓ Be committed to cultural exchange and be willing to welcome an au pair as a family member.

✓ Be U.S. citizens or permanent legal residents.

✓ Be fluent in English and speak English as the primary language in the home.

✓ Provide the au pair with a private bedroom (she can share a bathroom).

✓ Submit a completed application and two references .

✓ Have an in-home interview with an agency represen-tative.

✓ Be willing to comply with U.S. Department of State regulations.

✓ Be willing to arrange the au pair's schedule so that she works up to forty-five hours a week, up to ten hours a day.

There are 17.69 million working mothers of children under the age of 18 years in the United States. Nearly 8 million of these mothers have children under the age of 6. Whether they work full-time or part-time, and regardless of their chil-dren's ages, these women worry about the cost and quality of their childcare choices. Assuming they have a spare bed-room, the au pair program may just be the answer to their childcare problems.

CHAPTER 2:

MAIL-ORDER CHILD CARE

Having evaluated my childcare options, I saw many good things about having an au pair. The rules of employment were pre-set, including the pay, the hours, the vacation, and the benefits. My au pair would always show up in the morning. I liked the fact that I would hardly ever have to get a weekend babysitter. My kids would learn about other cultures without having to travel extensively. There was someone who could wait at home for the cable man to show up during the day. There would also be someone who could stay home at 9:00 at night if I had to run out to the grocery store to pick up the bottles of water I had promised to deliver to Field Day. It was decided; we were getting an au pair. I filled out the application and sent it off to the au pair agency, and we were soon approved to enter the host-family world. Then, we went au pair shopping.

Online Au Pair Shopping

Almost all the au pair agencies now have host families screen applicants on their Web sites using a catalogue of au pairs. To gain access to the listings, you have to first submit your application and be approved. You will always see beautiful pictures of beautiful young women with happy children playing games. Each agency has a different process for screening. Some allow host families to access all the applicants. Some agencies will only allow you to look at pre-selected candidates. In general, the Web sites are easy to navigate, and the host family can request candidates of a certain nationality or language. Other "filters" for searching include soonest arrival date, driving ability, swimming ability, and if the au pair is a smoker. Depending on what time of year you look, there will be more au pairs from some countries than others. There might be many from Germany and none from South Africa. It seems there are always au pairs available from Thailand and Brazil.

TIP: Ask your agency what time of year is best for the largest selection of au pair candidates.

On my agency's Web site, you will see photos of the au pairs and basic information: first name, country of origin, and earliest arrival date. You can click on their photos to see more, including their essays, photos, face-to-face interview forms, and driving abilities. As you read applications, you can "tag" a candidate as a "favorite." As you research the list, your "favorites" list will likely grow.

Remember that this is not Overstock.com. You can't just return an au pair that you don't like because she doesn't look the same as what you saw on the Web site. This is a long-term commitment. The au pair candidates are real people with complicated lives that are sometimes hard to see (or hidden) in their applications.

To get the fullest possible picture of the candidates, I like to get my whole family involved, though I have to admit that I am the one who becomes obsessed with looking for au pairs on the Web site. I read as many applications as I can, and I read every word. I look at every picture and read every detail on the application. I check the Web site several times a day to see if there are new additions.

Some au pairs say that they will only be placed in a certain city. If you like them, call them anyway. You can often change their minds. If you don't like any of the candidates on the Web site, call the agency directly. They can often link you to those who are not yet on the Web site, allowing you the first look at the newest candidates.

"I Love Children" and Other Little Lies on the Application

Choosing an au pair, someone who will live in your house and be entrusted with your children, is fundamentally an incredible leap of faith. But with proper preparation and a little private-eye sleuthing, you can have great confidence that you are hiring someone who will complement your family, be easy to live with, and provide excellent care for your children.

The au pair's application makes the first impression and is the one tool you have to decide which candidate is right for you. Depending on your agency, you will look at the complete application package either online or in paper copy. The agency that we use is highly automated. Think Match.com for child care.

You must learn how to decode and discern the various parts of the application to narrow the list of potential au pairs. Here is what is included in most application packages:
   ✓ A one-page essay
   ✓ Two pages of photos
   ✓ One page of biographical information
   ✓ One page of relevant facts
   ✓ A one-page listing of childcare experience
   ✓ Medical forms

✓ Childcare reference forms
✓ Au pair agency interview form

The Essay

The one-page essay reveals much about the applicant, but you have to read between the lines (and sometimes look in the margins). Some au pairs type. Some handwrite. Some adhere cutesy stickers of Disney characters, draw Winnie the Pooh, or sprinkle glitter all over them. However, most essays follow the same format: an introduction of who the applicant is and where she lives, followed by a long paragraph describing her childcare experience, and a closing paragraph about what she wants to accomplish by coming to the U.S.

You will read the same thing over and over again: "I want to be an au pair because I love children" or "I want to open a kindergarten." Ninety percent of the time, this is complete and utter crap. They might *like* children, but very few au pairs aspire to a career in child care.

The au pair's personality should come through in her essay. Read enough essays, and you will soon be able to tell if the candidate is energetic, playful, shy, serious, ambitious, or sporty. The essay is also a good indication of her English proficiency.

TIP: Au pairs who have difficulty with English use computer-based translating programs on their essays. Look for strange word usage as a clue if they are using these programs.

I like to see an essay where the au pair fesses up to her real motivation for joining the au pair program. Chances are she doesn't *really* want to open a kindergarten in her home country after she completes the program, so in the essay, I want to see the candidate honestly share her true dreams and aspirations—her real motivation for joining the au pair program.

I decided not to interview the au pair candidate who wrote the following essay (it was handwritten and surrounded by stickers of Snow White and the Seven Dwarves):

> *Dear Host family!*
> *My name is [X]. I enjoy spending all day with children because we always have fun. We went to the park, shooping, at cinema, rode a bicycle, etc. In this moment, first of all, I must study tourism and my rutine occupy lot of time. I believe I am a good housewife. To sump up, I know that I will have a good experience in America. I have spent very good moments with children and I know that they will have a good care too. Trust me! Good bye, [X]*

The above essay did not tell me anything about the girl's background or her childcare experience. Although the girl certainly seemed spirited (evidenced by the exclamation points!), she did not reveal her motivation for joining the program. And let's face it, her English is atrocious. If an au pair's written English is poor, her spoken English will be even worse.

The Photos
Next, look at the pages of photos. The photos are scanned and photocopied from the original paper application, so the quality of the photos varies tremendously. The first page is always full of pictures of the candidate with children. The second page is always pictures of family and friends.

Look for smiles in the pictures. You can learn a lot from them. Are the children smiling? Are the au pairs smiling? Are the family members smiling? Do the children look like they even know the au pair? Or did she grab some kids at a local playground and say, "Take pictures with me!"? Did she wear really high heels to play with children at the playground? Is she revealing her belly button? Is she wearing too much makeup? Any visible tattoos or body piercings?

If the girl looks happy in her photos, chances are she is a happy person. In the family photos, does everyone look affectionate and loving? These are qualities that you will look for in an au pair. If she looks sad or mad or is scowling, she is probably an angry person (and might not be so easy to live with). Do not choose a girl who is scantily clad, trying to look seductive or sexy in her pictures. There may be some serious judgment issues there.

The Relevant Facts
Next, you will review two pages of relevant facts about the au pair candidate. Does she drive? When did she get her driver's license? If she drives, is she comfortable driving in the snow? Will she live in a house with pets? (Most say that they will not live in a house with spiders or snakes.) Does she smoke? If so, is she a "social smoker"? What is her religion? Does she know how to swim? What are her hobbies? All au pairs check "handicrafts," though I'm not sure what that is.

If the au pair says that she is not comfortable driving in the snow and you live in Minnesota, do not interview her. If she says that she does not like dogs and you have a slobbery golden retriever, do not interview her. If you live in a house in Florida with an in-ground pool and the au pair can't swim, move on. There will be plenty of other applicants to look at.

Biographical Information
Next, check out the one-page biography. The au pair applicants will range from eighteen years old to twenty-six years old. Do not assume that the au pair candidate's age tells you anything about her maturity. Our nineteen-year-old au pair Elisa was the most mature au pair we ever had. Age does provide some facts that you can rely on, however. An older au pair will be less expensive to add to your car insurance than a younger au pair. A younger au pair will have less driving experience. Au pairs who are over twenty-one will be able to go to bars and nightclubs.

In the biographical information, you learn the occupations of the au pair's parents and if she has any siblings. This page also reveals if the candidate has ever lived away from home or has traveled outside her home country, if she has ever been to America before, and what level of education she has completed.

TIP: Look for an eldest sibling; they are often responsible for taking care of younger kids.

Look for an au pair who has lived away from home before, either at school or for a job. She will have a much easier adjustment to living in the U.S. She will have experienced homesickness before. She will know how to do her own laundry and cook her own meals. She will know what it is like to live away from her family. By choosing an au pair who has this life experience, you can be confident that your au pair will be somewhat self-reliant.

If you have boys, look for an au pair who has younger brothers. She will be familiar with LEGOs and conversant on *Star*

Wars. If you have girls, look for an au pair who has younger sisters. She will know all about *High School Musical* and be comfortable playing with dolls.

TIP: If you get pregnant and have a baby while you have an au pair and your au pair does not have the required "infant" hours, the agency is required by the State Department to remove the au pair from your house. If you think you might have another baby, chose an au pair who already has her "infant hours."

Childcare Experience

Next, look at the pages of childcare experience. Childcare experience is divided into two sections: au pairs with significant experience with children under the age of two and au pairs with experience with kids over the age of two. Experience can be defined as babysitting neighbors or family members or in a school setting. My experience is that many au pair candidates "volunteer" or "intern" at a day care, nursery school, or kindergarten setting as soon as they make the decision to become an au pair to get the needed hours of experience.

TIP: Just because an au pair has volunteered at a day care center does not mean that she loves children. Look for an au pair who has experience with children prior to making the decision to be an au pair.

Since the unfortunate Louise Woodward incident, all au pairs who are going to care for a baby must prove that they have at least two hundred hours of experience in caring for infants. This is vigilantly verified by the agency in their home countries.

Medical Forms
The medical forms reveal the weight and height of your au pair, assuming that you can translate from metric. For a second, I was sure our first au pair was going to be three feet tall and weigh 283 pounds. Fortunately, I was wrong. You will also learn that your future au pair is fully immunized. The key thing to look for on the medical form is allergies. Any au pair who is allergic to anything in her home country will be doubly allergic here.

Reference and Interview Forms
The final piece of the application package is the reference and interview forms. You will see written references from the au pair's previous employers and an interview form from the agency representative. However, these references are nearly always translated from a native language and therefore seem generic (i.e., completely useless).

Once you read forty or so applications, you will see that they all say the same thing: *"X is a lovely girl. She wants to be an au pair because she loves America, wants to learn about another culture, and wants to improve her English. She LOVES children! I would trust her to take care of my own."* The only takeaway from the reference and interview forms is that you can have confidence that an actual person, employed by your agency, met the candidate in person to verify the information in the application.

The List of Favorites
After reviewing dozens of applications, you will be drawn to several candidates for various reasons. Some candidates will

just click with you; there will be good chemistry. It might be the essay or the photos, her hobbies, religion, or life experiences. As you identify candidates you like, you build a list of "favorites." After building this list, you then have to choose two candidates to interview by telephone. Once you have chosen the two au pairs to interview, their online profiles will disappear from the Web site and become unavailable to other families for forty-eight hours. During those two days, you contact the candidates, conduct the telephone interviews, and make a judgment if you want to continue the interview process. After the forty-eight hours, your time expires and the candidates pop back up onto the Web site for other families to interview.

Candidates with strong applications will go quickly, so once you have made the decision to interview a candidate, move fast. Pull out your phone card and get on the phone. Just remember to dial 011 first.

Secrets of International Calling

Every time I have to find a new au pair, I buy myself an online phone card. Pinzoo has had my international calling business for some time now. It is a cheap and easy way of making calls to various countries.

Next, I always find out the time difference in the home country of the au pair and mark the front of her application in big Magic Marker—"+ 6 hrs," for example. It does not make a great first impression when you wake the au pair up at five in the morning.

I usually try to e-mail the candidate first to let her know that I will be calling. In the "introductory e-mail," I introduce myself and let her know a little bit about our family. I then let her know exactly when I will call. Hopefully then, she will be prepared for the call.

Sometimes she will respond right away to say that she has already matched or that she is interested in speaking on the phone. I never wait for a response. I always just call. Remember, you only have forty-eight hours before this candidate is back on the market. If she is a great candidate, you want to scoop her up.

On the application, the au pairs generally give both their home phone numbers and their cell phone numbers. Calling cell numbers is much more expensive than calling landlines. Keep that in mind.

TIP: Even though it is more expensive, call the candidate's cell phone first. These girls and guys are busy and hardly ever at home. You have a better chance of connecting on their mobiles.

If and when I actually connect with the au pair candidate, I always start the conversation with two questions:
"Is this a good time to talk?"
and
"Have you found a host family yet?"

One time, I called a girl from Norway who looked like the most perfect au pair I had ever seen. I was so excited to talk with her that I launched right into my pitch. "This is who we are. This is why you should be our au pair." About three minutes into my spiel, the au pair interrupted me and meekly said, "But, Nancy, I have already matched with another family." Damn, another one got away (not to mention all those minutes from the phone card).

The Beauty of an Open-Ended Question

When I make interview calls to potential au pairs in other countries, I always give the au pairs the benefit of the doubt. They have so much to overcome on that first call. English is not their first language, and speaking on the phone is difficult in another language, especially when there is so much information to take in and impart. They really have to think on their feet, so I always forgive them when they stumble over words and have trouble communicating.

You must determine quickly if the candidate's English level is adequate for you and your family, however. During one interview, we tried very hard to communicate with a beautiful blonde Brazilian girl who was a semi-professional surfer. My teenage son would have loved her, I am sure. But on the phone, it seemed she could not speak a word of English. I spoke to her and could tell that she was incredibly nervous. I tried to be reassuring. She panicked and put her mother on the phone. Mom's English was no better than the surfer girl's. The mother then put the brother on the phone. He actually did speak some English, but all I learned was that the surfer girl was very nervous about speaking on the phone. I should have just stopped right there. Instead, I enlisted the help of a friend's Brazilian au pair to translate for us. She used my entire Pinzoo card and assured me that the surfer girl would pick up English very quickly. I just couldn't go through with it. She was off the list. I moved on to the next applicant.

After you have established that "Yes, it is a good time to talk" and "No, I have not yet found a host family," you can delve into the meat of the matter. Ask open-ended questions during the phone interview. These are questions that cannot be answered with "yes" or "no" or one word.

The first phone call with our very first au pair, Vera, was torture. I had to force myself to speak very slowly and in short sentences. I cannot begin to describe how hard it is for me to do this. In return, Vera spoke deliberately. Her English was slow but steady. I could understand her, just barely. (Remember, I was a rookie at this point.)

Write out the questions you want to ask in advance. And take notes along the way. Once you make a dozen calls, you will forget who said what!

"Tell me about your family," I asked Vera, thinking this was a good open-ended question to start.

"I have a mother."

Pause.

"A father."

Longer pause. I held my tongue, trying to give her the time she needed to answer the question.

"And a brother," she answered.

Oh well, I thought. *Maybe I'll get more information with the next question.*

"Tell me about your job," I asked. Another decent open-ended question.

She answered, "I work."

Pause.

"In a factory."

Pause.

"The factory makes shirts."

Long pause.

"I sew shirts." Now we were getting somewhere. *She sews!*

I continued, "How old are you?" *Closed-ended question*, I thought. *Dammit!*

"I."

Pause.

"Am twenty-four years old," she answered. This was going nowhere!

"Why do you want to come to America?" I asked. *Open-ended question. OK*, I thought. *We are back on track.*

"Because I want to learn English."

Pause.

"Because I love children," Vera replied.

Now, this last answer, "because I love children," is one I've heard time and again. That and "because I want to start a kindergarten." There must be a secret au pair training guide telling the au pair that she must tell you that she "loves children" and that she wants to be a "teacher in a kindergarten," because every au pair that I have ever interviewed has given me that same stock answer. Only one of my fourteen au pairs has actually continued on to have a career in early childhood education. Nevertheless, being new to this whole routine, I thought Vera's answer was cute.

Make sure that your spouse also calls the candidate. Another point of view will help you to make an educated decision as to whether this au pair is right for your family. Mark talked to Vera. They talked about running. She ran five times per week, six to eight miles per day. She then biked to the factory for work (my God, it was almost a triathlon!). She was a hard worker and athletic. Her English was adequate. She said she loved children. She sounded nice. We matched. Vera ended up being an OK au pair. She was competent but cold. But she was our first au pair, and we learned a lot about cultural exchange.

Deal-Breaker Questions

Even though you are trying to sell yourself to the au pair candidate during the phone interview, you must ask her the tough questions. But first, ask *yourself* the tough questions. One such question is, "What would be the hardest part about living in my family?" If you do not have the answer to that question, ask a friend. Or ask your mother-in-law.

For me, two things come to mind. First, we have a really big dog. My kids are really easy; it's the dog that is often the deal breaker. So I need to know: Does the au pair candidate like dogs? Does she like big dogs? Has she ever had a dog? Would she agree to help care for a dog? Ask the question and then listen carefully to the answer. I learned this the hard way from our au pair Carla.

One day, I got a text message from Will on my phone when our dog, Ginger, was still a puppy. Attached to the message was a photo of my favorite chair in our living room. It was an armless chair, low to the ground, almost a stool with a comfy back, two cool carved faces on the corners, and claw feet. Only in the picture, it didn't look like a chair anymore. From the photo, I could see fabric strips pulled away from the seat cushion. I could see the springs, the stuffing, and fabric strewn across the living room floor. The chair was not valuable—we had picked it up at a garage sale years earlier—but it had great sentimental value. It was the perfect size for someone five feet flat. I loved that chair.

"What happened?" I texted to Will.

"Ginger!" he answered.

When I got home, Carla admitted that she had completely forgotten to put Ginger in her crate when she had gone out during the day, giving Ginger hours to dissect the chair. She was not apologetic. She did not say she was sorry. She just said that yes, she forgot to put Ginger in her crate. She did not even attempt to clean up the mess or hide the evidence. The dog and the dog's actions were clearly not something that Carla felt at all responsible for. She really did not like dogs.

The second deal-breaker question that I have to ask prospective au pairs is how they spend their free time. With our family (at least during the school year), our au pair has a ton of free time. One would think that this would be a good thing. Certainly as a working mom with two kids, I would absolutely adore six unscheduled hours every day. But for some reason, this can be difficult for a nineteen- or twenty-year-old.

For example, our eleventh au pair, Sabrina from Germany, was a great au pair. She immediately connected with the boys; she was neat; she made friends; she was a great driver

49

and could follow directions and read maps. I thought things were really going well, but then she announced to me that she had decided to go home six months early.

"Why?" I implored.

"I have too much time to think. Too much time alone," she explained. "I see you and your family, and you have such a nice life. And I think about my family and my boyfriend at home."

OK, now I got it. It was the boyfriend. Sabrina continued, "I want to go home and start to build my life so that one day it can be as perfect as your life."

"Perfect?" I responded. "My life is NOT perfect! You just quit!!"

I then realized that idle time is not necessarily good for all au pairs. Sabrina had too much time on her hands. She was brooding about the life she was "missing" in Germany. She was asking herself questions like, "Will my boyfriend wait for me? Will I get into the university in my hometown or somewhere far away? I wonder if these new sheets I just bought will match my bedroom walls."

Now, when I interview au pairs, I ask the tough questions. "How do you fill your free time? What do you do when you are bored? Do you have hobbies?" If they say shopping, then they are off the list. After three months, they will get sick of shopping and will just be bored. That is a recipe for disaster. Our most successful au pairs have been avid readers. I happily pick them up new books at Costco.

Regardless of your deal breakers, you should ask if the au pair has ever lived away from home before. Even a sleepaway summer camp will have prepared her for the feeling of homesickness and living with strangers. This will help with the transition.

After that first phone call interview, pause. Don't just move on to the next application. Ask yourself, "Does the au pair seem compatible with my family? Do I like her? Do I sense a connection? Shared values? Similar styles? Do I like the sound of her voice? Does she seem to like me? **Is there chemistry?**" This is so much like dating, it's frightening.

Also, how is her English? You have to give the candidates a little slack, but don't hang yourself. If the au pair says, "Can you e-mail me your questions?" this means that she can't really understand what you are saying. If she says that she is nervous and asks if you will speak to her brother or mother or sister, say no thank you and move on. Ask questions that she is not expecting—and may not have pre-written answers to. For example, ask what the weather is like or what she did on a recent holiday. This is a great way to test how good her English really is.

TIP: The two things that you must determine during that first call: Is there chemistry? How is her English?

Don't be cynical. But be realistic. If her level of English is very bad in the beginning, she will have a very hard time connecting with your children. It might improve, but by then, it might be too late.

Now it's your turn. Make a list of the deal-breaker questions for your family.

The Match Game

Once you have decided on an au pair, you must call her to extend the offer. This is called "matching," the term that is used when the au pair and the family commit to one another. As a family, we officially offer the job to the au pair, and the au pair accepts. Remember, we have never actually met this person. We have spoken to her on the phone, we have exchanged a dozen e-mails and lots of photos, but we have never laid eyes on her. She packs up, gets on a plane, and takes a very long flight to the United States to live with a family she has never met in person. It is an enormous leap of faith for both the au pair and the host family.

When I called Vera, our first au pair, to offer her the job, I was butterflies-in-the-stomach nervous.

"We would like to offer you the job as our au pair."

"I accept," was her reply.

The next decision is the arrival date. You need to carefully coordinate your schedule with the arrival dates offered by the agency. Generally, there are two or three arrival dates per month. The au pairs arrive in the United States on a Monday, attend a three-day training session, and are picked up by their host families on a Thursday.

Once you and the au pair decide on an arrival date, you inform the agency of the match officially by matching on the Web site. This action will permanently take the au pair off the market and officially begin your experience as a host parent. Once this is done, the arrival date cannot be changed.

TIP: The minimum time between matching with an au pair outside the country and when she can arrive is six weeks. If you are in a hurry, match with an "in-country" au pair.

After you match, you wait. It takes four to six weeks for your au pair to actually get to the U.S. In her home country, the au pair gets her affairs in order, applies for her International Driving Permit, and works with her agency to secure the visa that allows her to come to the U.S. This is no easy feat. Rarely, au pairs are denied visas by their home countries to come to the United States. The agencies work closely with the home countries to make sure that this happens as infrequently as possible; however, you may want to ask your au pair agency in which countries this might be happening and avoid matching with au pairs from there.

Each au pair must travel from her hometown to the nearest U.S. embassy or consulate to apply for the visa and undergo an interview. We have been told that the interviews in South Africa can be grueling. In Sweden, the process is a cakewalk.

As part of the preparation to come to the United States, each new au pair is required to complete an "orientation project." This mandatory book report includes information about the host family, the children, and the region and town in which she will be living, as well as information on her background. The project helps the new au pair to see herself as part of your family and learn more about American life. Just like her application, chances are, there will be cute stickers attached.

Be in contact with your new au pair frequently before she leaves her home country. E-mail her a lot. Send pictures and keep her up to date on family news. Remind her of things to pack (a warm jacket if you live in Chicago, bathing suits and sandals if you live in Florida). Encourage her to pack light. She will spend a lot of time shopping when she gets here and will need to buy another suitcase just to get home.

The Au Pair's First Days in the States

Monday is au pair arrival day. Almost all au pairs enter the United States through JFK Airport in New York City. The agencies then put them up in a hotel in or around New York and provide three days of "orientation," a requirement from the U.S. State Department. Our agency calls this "Au Pair Academy."

It may be an urban legend, but I have heard that once in a blue moon, an au pair will "disappear" at the airport or in New York and run off to some other intended destination, using the au pair program as a reason to enter the States. Others are just too homesick or too freaked out by their new world to stay, and they turn around and go home before even meeting their host families.

Au Pair Academy
Until recently, our agency used the New Yorker Hotel for Au Pair Academy. The New Yorker Hotel is located right next to Penn Station and Madison Square Garden, just down the street from the Macy's flagship store. The au pairs had breakfast, lunch, and dinner at the Tick Tock Diner in the lobby and browsed through the H&M store for really inexpensive underwear.

The agencies have gotten more organized regarding the au pairs' first days. The State Department requires the agencies to conduct an official curriculum performed by trained professionals. My agency holds "Au Pair Academy" in the suburbs, at a large Sheraton with only a skyline view of New York. Here, the au pairs are cooped up in conference rooms for training sessions, drink Starbucks coffee in the lobby, and are ferried to Manhattan for a double-decker bus tour.

During the day, the au pairs attend Au Pair Academy, the required three-day training program run by the agency. This "hands-on and interactive training program" covers the following topics:

✓ Support resources from the agency

✓ Review of childcare basics such as feeding and bathing

✓ Review of stages of child development

✓ CPR and first-aid training

✓ Tips for living with an American family

✓ Overview of the American culture

✓ How to care for more than one child at a time

✓ Driving in the U.S.

✓ Tips on how to make the most of the year

✓ American games and songs for children

✓ How to deal with an emergency

At night, the au pairs share a small room with several complete strangers who probably speak a different language. As you can imagine, the au pairs are seriously jet-lagged and homesick and can't get much sleep. I wonder if they pay much attention to the orientation at the academy.

Pickup Day
Thursday is pickup day. Around noon, all the au pairs going to other states are ferried to NY airports for connecting flights to Chicago, San Francisco, Houston, and Atlanta, where they will begin their year of cultural exchange. When you pick up your au pair, you must show photo ID to the au pair agency representative, who will then release the au pair to your custody.

Those of us in the New York area meet our au pairs in the lobby of the hotel. Between the appointed hours of 2 p.m. and 5 p.m., the au pairs sit on their luggage, gnaw on their fingernails, chat nervously with their new friends, chew gum, drink coffee, and eye suspiciously any and all who enter the revolving doors. As a host family, you walk through those doors with equal unease. Which one is she? How is her English, really? Will she wear too much perfume? Too much makeup? Will she have bad breath? Will my kids like her? Will she have a really, really heavy suitcase?

We have had some memorable pickups.

The whole family traveled to New York City to pick up Vera. It was about 4:30 p.m. when we piled through the revolving doors and entered the lobby of the New Yorker Hotel. There we found Vera, a petite, muscular girl with short, hennaed hair and severely plucked eyebrows. She had one large suitcase and a shy smile. We warmly welcomed her and stumbled through our greetings. Mark lugged her suitcase to the parking garage, and we all piled into the Volvo wagon (at the time unblemished and almost new). Vera sat in the middle of the backseat atop discarded Cheerios and dog hair in between the boys in their booster seats. It took us more than an hour to get through the Lincoln Tunnel, all the time making small talk, asking about family, friends, where she wanted to travel, what she wanted to see. Along about Thirty-fourth Street and Tenth Avenue, Mark and I noticed that her English was not very good. During a lull in the conversation, I took a deep breath. She was really nervous and wore a lot of perfume; her breath seemed fine.

Our second au pair, Kit, arrived in the dead of winter, having never seen snow before. Pickup day was a clear, crisp, sunny January day, and we brought the boys into the city, so they were in a particularly good mood. We headed to the New Yorker Hotel with high hopes that this match would be a great one. We parked the Volvo in the garage next to the New Yorker Hotel and all piled into the lobby to find Kit. She was easy to spot at about 5'5" tall, with blonde curly hair cut in a short bob, and at about 195 pounds. She was cheerful, funny, and a little awkward, and we laughed a lot on the ride home. Mark had been to Australia recently, and they compared notes on the very long flight to New York. Wedged between the two booster seats in the backseat, she was making the kids laugh. I was relieved to have such a nice beginning.

It was Andrea's bad fortune to arrive in New York City during the coldest month in a century. It was the kind of weather that made you wish for global warming. The poor girl had never seen snow before, much less been in temperatures below zero. The day I had to make the annual pilgrimage to the New Yorker Hotel was dismal, so I decided to leave the boys at home with Mark. It was too cold to schlep them to the city. It was bitter, windy, cold, and dark when I walked into the lobby of the New Yorker Hotel to meet Andrea for the first time. There she was, one of the last au pairs in the hotel, with a thin wool coat, a black crocheted knit cap, and thin knit gloves. She was shivering.

"Andrea?" I ventured toward her.

"Nancy?" she answered. Her cheeks were bright red and matched her red lipstick.

"Yes!" I replied. "What a day! It is so cold out! Welcome! How are you? How was your orientation?" We exchanged small talk. I kept the conversation upbeat and energetic, trying hard to get things off on the right foot.

"The car is just around the corner in the garage next to the hotel. It's not a long walk. Can I help with your bags?" I offered. Andrea gave me her huge, heavy suitcase to carry while she carried her backpack and handbag. I lugged the suitcase and me down the ice-covered street to the parking garage.

I struggled to find things to talk about on the way home. I asked simple, open-ended questions and spoke slowly. Andrea's English was not good, and seeing how prim she was, I worried about how she would connect with the kids. Thirty minutes later, as we inched our way to the entrance of the Lincoln Tunnel, I turned to look at my new au pair in the passenger seat. Even with the heated seats and the blower on high, Andrea shivered the whole way home.

 TIP: Give your au pair the front seat on the way home. Doing so will help her to begin to figure out exactly where she is.

Bobby arrived during the first week of December. As usual, we headed to the New Yorker Hotel. This time, Mark and I did the pickup without the boys, who were home, preparing for Bobby's arrival with KiKi, who was staying to help Bobby's adjustment. I arrived to the lobby of the New Yorker

Hotel before Mark. Whoa. Bobby was hard to miss. Six foot six, shaved head, blue eyes, striking jaw. He looked Scandinavian, with a distinctively urban bent. He wore baggy, really baggy, jeans. He had a look like a modern Vanilla Ice. Is there such a thing as a German rapper? There must be. Boy, Bobby was handsome. He and I sat in the lobby of the New Yorker Hotel, waiting for Mark, who was running late. We talked about the orientation and the other au pairs. Bobby had brought a lot of luggage, including his bicycle, a fancy motocross bike. I could tell he was nervous because he played with his hands, rubbing his fingertips constantly against the base of his thumbs. But he smelled good. His English was great. He was shy but nice, and oh my, he was very good-looking.

When Mark arrived, we all walked to the parking garage. Bobby carried his large suitcase. Mark carried Bobby's motocross bike in its travel case. With at least eighteen inches on me, Bobby could not sit in the backseat of the car with his knees jammed in the front seat, so I offered Bobby the front seat, and he and Mark talked most of the way home. I sat in the back and picked Cheerios off the seats.

We arrived home to a big "Welcome Bobby" sign the boys had made and taped to the front door.

TIP: Have your kids make a big welcome sign and put it on the door of your house. It makes a really good first impression.

59

The Presentation of Gifts

The secret au pair handbook that instructs the au pairs to say that they "love children" also recommends that they bring gifts to their new families, much as the ancients made offerings to appease their gods. From each au pair, we have had the ritual presentation of gifts.

Discuss with your au pair in advance what she will bring for the children. A great gift from your au pair to your child will help to establish that much-needed connection. Chocolate is always a winner in my family.

Vera presented us with carefully wrapped packages in traditional Slovakian gift wrap. The boys got books, candy, and small toys. Hank dove right into the Slovakian chocolate. Will tried the fruit-flavored chewy candy and went directly to the wastebasket and spit it out. Mark and I received a beautiful crystal vase that I still use today.

Lena brought a DVD about the Czech Republic (and candy). Helen brought a book about Bergen, Norway (and candy). Sabrina brought Hank a stuffed animal, Will a LEGO, and us German chocolate.

Even though she was our worst au pair, Carla gave us the best presents: two wonderful handcrafted wooden Buddhist statues. She called them "grandmother" and "grandfather," and they represented spirits that protect a family. I thought they were cool. For the boys, she brought candy. They were psyched.

After matching with our au pair, Elisa, I made suggestions via e-mail on the gifts: for Hank, a stuffed animal; for Will, a CD of a famous Swedish rock band; for Mark and me, chocolate (what else?). It was a hit, all around. Hank named his new lion "Leyon" (lion in Swedish) and slept with it every night for a month after Elisa's arrival. The connection was made immediately.

Greet your new au pair with a gift. I give each of our new au pairs a "welcome" card, holding three or four gift cards of $10 or $15 from Starbucks, the local ice cream shop, the movies, and the bookstore. I want them to get out of the house and meet friends, and if they are not spending their own money, they might just do it.

CHAPTER 3:

LESSONS FOR LIVING WITH THE LIVE-IN

What is it like with an au pair actually living in your house? Do you treat your au pair like a houseguest? Like a family member? Or like an employee? The secret to a successful au pair–host family relationship is a delicate combination of all three. The balance you create will depend a lot on the style of your family. So be honest with yourself and your au pair about how your family functions. That will be the beginning of a great year together.

This chapter provides you with the knowledge needed to achieve that delicate balance. The following lessons are essential for a successful relationship with an au pair and will help to create a smooth transition into a great year together.

Recognize the Five Stages of Au Pair Adjustment

It takes a full five weeks for the family and au pair to fully adjust to the new situation. Do not to expect too much to begin, with but don't to be too lax, either. This is an emotional time for the au pair but also a very important period in which to determine whether her skills and style match well with your family.

I soon became familiar with and am now prepared for the five weeks of au pair adjustment. When your au pair arrives, prepare for the following:

Week One
This is a week of excitement. The kids are friendly. The host parents are forgiving. The au pair is busy learning the routine,

getting to know her new family, unpacking her s
sonalizing her room, adjusting to driving a big car,
ing the street maps. You are full of hope. Enjoy it.

One rite of passage in my house during week one is the
trip to the grocery store. Here, I get a sense of what sort
food the au pair likes so I can keep it on the weekly list.
Almost every one of our au pairs has fallen in love with
potato bread (think sweet yellow Wonder Bread), Oreo cookies, and peanut butter. Keep plenty on hand; comfort food
will help ease the transition.

During week one, we drive around the town so I can show the
new au pair where the Starbucks is, where the movie theater
is, where the YMCA is, and where to park. I am sure to show
her the different au pair hangouts, such as the sandwich shop,
the diner, and the local pubs (if she's over twenty-one, of
course).

Also during week one, I take the au pair to a big home store
to get her a few things to personalize her room. Sally got
some funky pillows for her bed. Sabrina got a hanging shoe
rack and a full-length mirror. Most au pairs really care about
making their rooms special. Some even bring stuff from
home, like sheets and pictures for the wall. I try to be accom-
modating, short of redecorating for each one.

---

*TIP: Set aside time each week to sit down with your
au pair to check in, review schedules, answer questions, and offer encouragement.*

Week Two
During the second week, depression and homesickness set in.
The au pair now fully realizes that she is really far from

., The food is different, the water tastes different, and the vision programs are in a completely foreign language. little is familiar to her. At the same time, the host parent completely forgets that the au pair needs attention and quickly gets back to her daily routine. At 7:00 a.m. sharp, I give a quick "Bye-bye! Have a great day!" and am out the door, leaving the au pair to look at the kids and think, *Now what do I do?*

A good au pair will motivate herself to get to know the kids, get out of the house, meet other au pairs, and sign up for the YMCA. The bad au pair will sequester herself in her room, call home a lot, and spend way too much time on the computer. If you find your au pair beginning to isolate herself, encourage her to get out, meet other au pairs for coffee or drinks, or go to the movies.

We went wrong with Vera during week two. Every day when I got home from work, she would disappear upstairs to her bedroom. I think she was doing crunches and push-ups. I would ask her if she was OK, and she would say robotically, "Yes, Nancy." We grew to calling the third floor of our house "the biosphere." Vera would go upstairs after I got home and not break the seal of the biosphere to come downstairs until 6:45 the next morning. It is no wonder Vera never gained a pound. The only thing I remember her eating that whole year was Light n' Lively yogurt—at a whopping ninety calories per serving. Looking back, I realize that I should have encouraged her to get out of the house more. I should have been nosier.

Also during week two, the coordinator comes for a visit to check in with both the au pair and host parent(s); this meeting is called the orientation. The coordinator reinforces several rules with the au pair, reminding her to call 911 in an emergency, to never drink and drive, and to always drive with her International Driving Permit in case she is pulled over by a policeman. The coordinator has a private chat with the au pair to see if she is homesick, if she is miserable, if she is communicating with the host parents, and if she is getting along with the kids. With the host parent(s), the coordinator checks in to find out how the au pair is connecting with the kids and how things are going. If things have been rocky, now is the time to document it with the coordinator. You might need the proof later on.

TIP: Stock your au pair's bathroom with more than just essentials. In addition to cleaning supplies and toilet paper, provide cold medicine, tissues, shampoo, sunscreen, dental floss, etc.

The orientation affords the opportunity to look for those telltale signs there might be a problem. I knew things were bad with Carla during the orientation with the local coordinator a full week after she arrived. When the coordinator asked her to describe the daily schedule, Carla could not remember the names of my children!

Week Three

This is when all my au pairs have gotten a cold—regardless of what time of year it is. Symptoms include frequent headaches and a runny nose. She will complain that she is tired all the time. Tell her to take Advil and drink lots of water. Buy her lots of Kleenex. Don't baby her, and make sure she keeps working. She will be fine in a few days.

Bobby was the only au pair who couldn't kick the week-three cold. This was because his cold symptoms were actually allergies. Serious allergies. Bobby was highly allergic to dust mites and informed me that his room was full of them. I bought him new pillows and sheets. He upped his daily dose of allergy medicine, and his mother sent him special spray to kill the dust mites. After a few days, he adjusted.

Also during the third week, the au pair must visit the nearest Social Security office to file the paperwork for a Social Security number. Why does your au pair have to get a Social Security number? Why, to pay taxes, of course! A Social Security number will also make it easier for your au pair to open a bank account, register for classes at the local university, and apply for a driver's license. To file, the au pair will need her passport and visa, as well as a special letter to the Social Security Administration from the sponsoring agency (the au pair agency). This letter is sent directly to the host family prior to the au pair's arrival. So don't lose it!

Week Four
Your au pair will start experiencing physical changes. Her face will completely break out in pimples, and she may gain weight. You see, your au pair has been eating Oreos and potato bread since she arrived. The water is different; the soap is different; and, besides, she is completely stressed out. You should tell her to drink a lot of water and go to the gym. Buy fresh fruit. And make sure she keeps working. This too shall pass (probably).

When faced with this shocking new development, don't let your au pair buy a year's supply of the ProActive skin care regimen sold by Jessica Simpson on her infomercial. About six weeks after Sabrina from Germany arrived, a large box was delivered to our house. It was the first month's shipment of a year's supply of ProActive. By then, her face had straightened itself out and she was completely pimple-free.

Week Five
The routine is in place. You should be in a good groove. Your au pair should have friends and be going out. She might complain that she has gained weight, but she should be happy, and you should be communicating well. The laundry should be done. The kids should be clean and fed. By week five, you will know for sure if the match is going to stick. And technically, the au pair agency is going to make you wait that long before requesting a rematch anyway. Experience has proven that the first few weeks are the toughest. If at the end of week five, everyone is happy, you are home free (probably).

Allow the Au Pair to Connect with the Kids: Leave Them Alone

It is vitally important that the au pair and the kids connect in the first few days. If by the end of the five weeks, your kids are still complaining or your au pair is still complaining, you've got a problem on your hands. As hard as it may seem, to foster the au pair–child connection, you must leave them alone together. Your au pair doesn't stand a chance of connecting with your children as long as you are in the house, eavesdropping on their conversations or checking out their play. Your kids must understand as soon as possible that you trust your au pair and that she is in charge. Go back to work. Schedule a date with your spouse. Go shopping. Get out.

When Karen arrived after we rematched, I had to immediately get back to a normal work schedule. I was relieved to see that Karen had connected with my kids after just a few short days. Proof positive came one day when I walked in the front door after work and heard Christmas carols blaring on the Bose. Karen and the boys were dancing in the kitchen to a choreographed version of "Jingle Bells."

Your kids' ages and the au pair's English proficiency have a lot to do with this connection. For my boys (who are now on the older side), being able to communicate verbally is the single most important factor in establishing and building a strong relationship with their au pair. If you have an infant, toddler, or younger child, then English proficiency will not necessarily affect their relationship. They will connect through play. It might hinder your relationship with your au pair, but it probably won't hinder theirs. Send them to the playground, often.

TIP: Buy a game of Twister. This is an excellent activity for someone who does not speak English well.

Kit connected with my boys from her very first day in the house. Why? She got on the floor and played with the kids. She liked the same television shows that they liked, especially the shows on Nickelodeon. She laughed at the same jokes they thought were funny. She played with their toys (and like them, she left them on the floor when she was done). She loved their games. And if she would have read a book, it would have been the same book. At eighteen, Kit was a big kid.

TIP: Remind your children that it is their responsibility, too, to be supportive of your au pair. Try to help them understand how hard it might be for your au pair to communicate. Encourage them to include the au pair in their lives.

Let's face it: Au pairs are put in a tough situation. They are plopped into a family dynamic and asked to both establish themselves as authority figures and be nice enough so the kids will be happy with them and not scream for "mommy" all day. The au pair must make this connection quickly, because if she fails to connect with the children in the first several weeks, the whole year is lost.

A good au pair must represent the will and desires of the parents, and yet, she must also be able to build a rapport with the kids that leads to trust. Every au pair has to find her own way of getting the kids to behave. For some au pairs, especially when their English is not perfect, this can be really hard. A good au pair has to figure out a way to be both good cop and bad cop, and do this quickly. I know from my experience as a nanny that this is not easy.

Andrea, a highly competent and educated young woman, was the first au pair we had who just did not make the connection. She made a fatal mistake in her first week: She forced my kids to eat a dinner that was completely foreign to them.

Later, Carla was an even bigger disaster. The twenty-two-year-old from South Korea simply did not understand English when it came out of the mouths of my boys. I could understand her, and she could understand me (because I forced myself to speak really slowly). But communicating with my boys was a different story. She did not understand them. They did not understand her. The result was that the boys completely ignored her. Carla spent time in a different room from the kids—not ignoring them, but keeping her distance. The boys subsequently got into trouble.

The agency and the local coordinator will tell you that, with patience and work, the au pair's English will improve quickly, and trust me, it does. But if the au pair and the kids haven't connected on some level, it might be too late.

Sign Your Au Pair up for English Lessons

I am not a linguist, but I think English must be the hardest language to learn. We have had au pairs with varying levels of English, and each dealt with it in a different way. Most eventually got to the point where they could communicate. If they did not, we rematched.

You do not need an au pair who is fluent in English (who speaks expertly without an accent), but you do need someone who is proficient in English. She must be able to communicate with you *and* your children. She must be able to hold conversations with many different people (other babysitters, the delivery man, the kid's teacher), and she must have command of a large vocabulary. As a proficient speaker, she will probably speak with an accent, but she should be able to understand, speak, and write clearly. Before your au pair arrives, you should prepare your children to listen for the accent and let them know that in the beginning, they may have to try hard to understand her. Remind them to speak slowly.

One of my biggest criticisms of the au pair agencies is that they do nothing in the application process to evaluate a candidate's ability to speak English. Just like at an English-as-a-second-language (ESL) school, it seems to me that candidates could be interviewed and "ranked" for their proficiency in English. Alas, this is up to you, prospective host parent. From your telephone conversations and from your correspondence, you must come to your own conclusions about your future au pair's English. Good luck. It's a puzzle.

As soon as she arrives, ask your au pair if you can correct her when she makes a mistake. Be gentle, of course. Then correct her, a lot. Tell your kids (if they are old enough to do so tactfully) to correct your au pair, too.

TIP: Buy a few Harlequin romance books and leave them in your au pair's room.

Several of my au pairs took English lessons while they were here. Vera took an ESL course at the local adult school, which included one night per week in the classroom with strict instruction and one night per week of casual conversation with volunteers. This approach worked. Vera arrived with almost no English, but she coped by being very observant and by keeping lists of words she didn't know on a yellow legal pad. She would occasionally ask me what specific words meant. She also learned by reading. Over the course of her year with us, Vera read hundreds of books, in English. In the beginning, it was mostly trashy romance novels. She then graduated to more challenging books, such as Agatha Christie novels. Vera mastered comprehension through reading. Her problem was that she didn't want to speak unless she knew it was perfect. This meant that she didn't speak much to us. It was a quiet year.

Hold off spending any money on English classes until after week five. You should know that the match will work out before making that investment.

Carla was our biggest challenge. Carla could communicate well enough in written English, but her comprehension skills were nonexistent. I would speak slowly to her, but her responses just didn't connect to the questions I was asking. I would ask her, "Do you understand?" She would answer, "Yes, Nancy!" Most of the time, I did not believe her one bit.

I began to communicate almost everything to Carla verbally and then again in writing. Before I left in the morning, I would write the day's schedule on an index card. When I got to work, I would send her an e-mail repeating myself. We had several miscommunications around playdates, after-school activities, and Ginger, our dog.

After about a week, I signed Carla up for intensive English classes at a for-profit school in New York City for the next ten Saturdays. From ten in the morning until four in the afternoon, Carla would be in an ESL class with eight or nine other students, and she would learn English. I was sure of it. It ended up being a waste of money. Carla and the kids never connected. She made some bad decisions, and we rematched.

My experience is that the au pairs from the Scandinavian countries (Sweden, Norway, and Denmark) have great English. The German and Austrian au pairs are also often close to being fluent English speakers. But the au pairs I have interviewed from France and Switzerland did not speak English well. Most au pairs from the Eastern European countries have adequate English, and they pick it up quickly. I have found that the countries to worry about are Brazil, Thailand, Korea, and Turkey. Interview carefully.

To speed up your au pair's comfort with speaking English, make sure that she has friends from other countries. If English is the only language that the au pairs have in common, then they will use it. Encourage her to go out with friends often. Also encourage your au pair to read aloud to your children, and encourage your children to read aloud to your au pair. They will learn the language together.

Write It Out: The Au Pair Handbook

Even though I think our household routine and house rules are pretty simple, I have discovered that there is nothing better than written instructions to reinforce the message. It took me until our third au pair to realize just how specific I had to be with my au pair about the details of the job. It's not rocket science, but you do need to provide a very detailed manual. (See Sample Manual in the appendix.)

For example, the day that Kit said her good-byes and left us after her year, I went upstairs to the third-floor au pair suite to see how it looked. Ouch. It was scary. She had not vacuumed her room the entire year. The beds were unmade. Had she ever changed the sheets? The wastepaper basket was overflowing. There were empty shopping bags everywhere. There were half-drunk soda cans on her dresser and candy wrappers on the floor. In the corner, she had left three large garbage bags filled with old clothes—her clothes. She must have completely changed her wardrobe over the course of the year.

Then I walked—with much trepidation—into the bathroom. Yuck. The shower/bathtub was disgusting. The ring around the tub was not so much a ring—the tub now looked two-toned: white on top and grayish brown on the bottom. There was blonde curly hair in the drain and half a dozen empty shampoo and conditioner bottles on the ledge. The shower curtain liner was covered in gunk. The sink and the toilet were in the same condition as the tub. I shuddered, closed the door, and left.

Hadn't I told her that it was her responsibility to clean her room? I think I had.

I knew I had to face the mess sooner rather than later. We were picking up our next au pair in a few days, and the room had to be clean. I returned to the third floor with a face mask and rubber gloves to clean, scour, and scrub. Several loads of laundry and garbage bags later, I emerged, and the room and the bathroom were clean again. I drove her old clothes in the garbage bags to a metal receptacle emblazoned with "CLOTHES FOR THE NEEDY" and dumped them in, sincerely hoping that she had washed them.

From then on, I was abundantly clear—in writing—with my au pairs about who was supposed to clean the third floor of our house: They were. Not me.

Our manual has evolved throughout our time with our fourteen au pairs. It now stands at about a twenty-page document that includes all details of our family routine, our lives, and our house. I give it to my new au pair on the day she arrives in the house. We then review it together, page by page.

I am constantly amazed at the level of detail that I must go into in the written instructions:

> *"Make sure that the clothes are right-side-out when you fold the laundry and put it away."*

Sabrina would put away clothes that were clean and inside out. Eight-year-old Hank would then put on his clothes, oblivious to the fact that they were inside out. On days when I left the house early, he would then walk to school with his shirt inside out.

"Remember to put soap in the dishwasher when you run it. The dishwasher soap is underneath the kitchen sink."

Karen hated loading and unloading the dishwasher and would regularly run the dishwasher without soap.

"You may not park in front of a fire hydrant. You must park the car in the direction of the street. You must put coins in the parking meter."

Bobby was a bad parker.

"Please put Ginger (the dog) in her crate when you leave the house."

I lost my favorite chair one day—as well as numerous shoes, stuffed animals, and a few pieces of homework—because Carla forgot to put Ginger in her crate when she left the house.

"The boys may not watch movies that are rated PG-13. Please look on the DVD case to see what the movie is rated. The children may watch DVDs that are rated G or PG. They may not watch movies that are rated PG-13 or R."

Lena let the boys watch the PG-13-rated movie *xXx* one day while she slept on the couch.

Take Your Au Pair Grocery Shopping

During the first week or so after a new au pair's arrival, I take her to the grocery store to have her show me what she likes, and I adjust the weekly grocery list accordingly.

75

TIP: Take your au pair grocery shopping and iden-
tify those foods that make her happy. Buy lots.

When Bobby was our au pair, I had to not only adjust my grocery list but also my grocery budget. I would buy two huge
boxes of Kellogg's Corn Flakes per week. And sure enough,
both boxes would be gone in days. I would buy boxes and
boxes of pasta, jars of sauce, apples and oranges by the bag-
ful, and gallons of milk and orange juice. I thought, *Oh my*
God, is this what it is like to have a teenage boy? And in not
so many years, I will have two of them. I was terrified. We
bought a membership at Costco.

TIP: Male au pairs eat more than female au pairs.
Adjust your grocery budget if you have a male au
pair.

After Carla arrived, I took her grocery shopping. First, we
went to an American grocery store. She walked the aisles,
looked carefully at labels, and did not choose one thing. I
bought potato bread. And Oreos. Just in case. Next, we went
to an Asian grocery store in the next town over. The East West
Market was a conglomerate of cultures and tastes. There were
fresh and packaged foods from Indonesia, Japan, China, Viet-
nam, India, and Korea. There was an aisle just for rice—sacks
and sacks, each from a different country, in large, medium,
small, and gigantic sizes. The brightly colored, plastic woven
sacks of rice had large lettering each in its respective language. There was an aisle for sauces and one for dried noodles. There were bags of rice snacks and sesame snacks, each
with a different country of origin. There were aisles of china

bowls and plates and of chopsticks and brightly colored dolls and toys. There were bins of bamboo flip-flops and comic books. The place smelled spicy.

As we walked the shopping cart up and down the aisles, Carla meticulously combed the shelves, picking up cans, reading the labels, and putting them right back on the shelf. She spent ten minutes inspecting the sacks of rice. After thirty minutes in the store, she did not have one item in the cart. Now, I can buy almost $200 in groceries in about twenty minutes, so I was wondering what was going on. I couldn't stand it any longer and had to ask.

"Carla, is there a problem? Why aren't you finding any-thing?" I asked.

"Not much food from Korea," she told me. "This is not good market."

I was losing my patience. It all looked pretty darn good to me. Wasn't it close enough? Couldn't she make do? Apparently, of the fifteen varieties of rice available, not one met with her satisfaction. In the end, she settled for some instant noodle soups and some frozen dishes. She did not pick up one single bag of rice. She said that she would keep looking.

> *TIP: In the interview process, ask the au pair can-didate if she eats a special diet and if she will require special food. If you cannot accommodate this request, do not match with that au pair.*

Some au pairs will have healthy diets, and some will be junk foodies. All au pairs are constantly on the lookout for food from home. Kit from New Zealand was thrilled to find a food shop for foods from England. When KiKi had friends visit from Japan, they came with suitcases full of nori and Japanese vinegar. When Karen's mother came to visit, she brought fig jam. Shortly after Elisa arrived, she made a bee-line for IKEA and stocked up on Swedish meatballs and boy-senberry jam.

If you are an organized host parent and can make a compre-hensive grocery list, you can ask your au pair to do the gro-cery shopping. I have never been quite good enough at making the list, but I know au pairs who do the weekly shop-ping for their host families. The checkout can be handled a number of ways: from giving the au pair a credit card for the weekly shopping to pre-purchasing store gift cards to giving the au pair cash.

Don't Expect Your Au Pair to Help with Homework

My au pair is responsible for overseeing homework time, but she is not a tutor. She will review the list of assignments and then make sure that Will and Hank actually complete them, but it has been the rare au pair who has ever been able to actu-ally help the kids with their homework.

Clarify what role you want your au pair to take in the kids' homework.

I remember when Will was in second grade and Kit was our au pair. In our school district, this was the first year for lots of homework. Most days, Will came home from school with one page of math problems to do, some reading, and a writing assignment. Luckily, reading and math came easily to Will, and there were rarely homework meltdowns. He was confident, efficient, and thorough about his schoolwork. He would march in from school, plop himself down at the kitchen table, and get to work. Kit would get him (and herself) a snack and look over his shoulder to make sure he was working on the problems. At least that is what I thought was happening. In fact, Will was teaching Kit how to do math.

One assignment was "boxes and arrows." You have to find the pattern. In one box there might be the number two, for example. Next to it was an arrow, and in the next box, there would be the number six, followed by another arrow, and in the final box would be the number ten. The exercise required that you figure out the pattern (add four, in this case). One late afternoon, I watched Kit as she sat next to Will with her head in her hands, concentrating on the problem.

"Look, Kit," Will said, "in this box there is a seven. The pattern tells me that I should add three. This means that I should put what number in the box next to the arrow?"

"Ten?" Kit guessed.

"Good," said Will as he filled in the number ten.

"And now look at these boxes and arrows. In this box, there is a ten, and the arrow points to a box that has a six. So what is the pattern?" he asked.

Kit concentrated.

"Take away four?" she asked.

"Good!" he shouted as he patted her on the head. This was Will's sign of affection to Kit. He would pat the blonde curls on the back of her head whenever he was proud of her or happy with something she did. She always smiled when he did this.

Will loved doing homework with Kit because he was the teacher and she was the student. I am just thankful that the homework wasn't algebra.

Get Your Au Pair a Cell Phone

Since the invention of the "family plan," we have gotten our au pair a cell phone. The schools have her number and know that she is the first person to call if one of the kids needs to be picked up from school. I feel better knowing that I can find her whenever I need her, and it gives me the confidence to let her go off during the day to the mall, to New York City, or over to a friend's house. Like parking and laundry, you have to be painfully clear with your au pair about the rules of the phone. I learned this the hard way.

> *Get a cell phone for your au pair, but make sure that it cannot dial or text internationally. Specify how many minutes and how many text messages she is allowed. Be clear with the au pair if you will make her pay the overage should she use more than the minutes allowed.*

Lena was a really good text messager. I had not yet been exposed to the ease and prolific use of text messaging prior to Lena's arrival in my home. Nor did I realize how expensive text messages could be. She was excited to get a new American cell phone (provided by me). She had it with her all the time and could text message with one hand (even while driving!). I noticed her texting skills but did not think anything of it until the next phone bill arrived. She had text messaged the Czech Republic three hundred times during the previous month, going over the plan by over two hundred messages. The bill was well over $400. I considered asking her to pay for a portion of it but ultimately just paid it and called the carrier to remove the feature that allowed her to text internationally.

Au pairs are very resourceful when it comes to staying connected to family and friends back home. They use VoIP connections, such as Skype, and instant messaging. These are relatively inexpensive and keep your au pair in touch with home.

Do Not Let Your Au Pair Drive Your Brand-New Volvo

Driving is one of the biggest issues between au pairs and their host families. Our big cars, automatic transmissions, multi-level parking decks, and congested roadways are huge challenges for these young people with little driving experience. As part of the requirements to come to the United States, they must obtain an International Driving Permit, but this does not guarantee that they are good drivers.

In some countries, au pair candidates can buy their International Driving Permit without ever proving that they can actually drive a car. When interviewing au pairs, you should ask very specific questions about their driving experience. (See sample questions in the Interview Checklist in the appendix.)

New Drivers

At seventeen, I had two fender benders within the first six months of getting my driver's license. I drove into the edge of the garage in my mother's Volkswagen. And then I really got into big trouble when I almost took the door off my father's big old diesel Mercedes. I backed out of the garage with the door still open! He is still mad at me over that.

So I should have known better when we matched with our second au pair, Kit. She was just eighteen years old and had been driving for only three months when she arrived in the United States. Not to mention the fact that she had been driving on the South Island of New Zealand, where her chances of hitting a stray sheep were greater than of hitting another car. Driving on the congested suburban roads and highways of New Jersey was not at all like navigating around the Kiwi countryside.

Arrange for an auto-pay system with a gas station, such as Exxon/Mobile's Speedpass, or get your au pair a gas credit card. This will make it easier for your au pair to fill up the car with gas.

After dinner one night, Kit asked to take our unblemished Volvo wagon to meet some friends for coffee. She cheerfully toddled out the back door to the car, and I heard the car start up from where I was sitting in the dining room. Volvos have a very distinctive purr to them, especially when the car is in reverse. As I sat at the dining room table, I listened to Kit back the car out of the driveway and then heard a crunch as the side of the car collided with the brick foundation of our house. I stood up and looked out the window, and there was Kit, sitting in the driver's seat, her head bowed on the steering wheel in shame, the car smooshed against the side of the house. She looked up through the sunroof and saw me looking down at her from the window. Slowly, she turned her head to look forward, put the car in drive, and inched it back into its parking place in the back of the house. The damage had sounded worse than it was. It wasn't horrible. Not worth getting fixed. Kit cried and cried, feeling incredibly guilty about it. She then called a friend and waited out front to be picked up.

So began a series of small but significant incidents, each one taking a small chunk out of the resale value of our Volvo. Do not allow your au pair to drive an expensive foreign car. If you own cars that you don't want damaged, consider buying an inexpensive used car for your au pair to drive.

Drive with each au pair before she actually takes your children out in the car. If you don't like the way she drives, get her driving lessons.

Carla was the worst au pair driver ever. Sitting expectantly in the passenger seat for our first drive, I watched Carla adjust the driver's seat of the Volvo to its most forward position so her knees were tucked right behind the steering wheel. She turned the car on, and then I saw the cardinal sin of driving. Carla put her left foot on the brake and her right foot on the accelerator.

"Stop," I said calmly before she could put the car in drive.

"In America, we only use our right foot to drive a car. Do you understand?" I asked. Carla's English was terrible, and I had to speak slowly and simply.

"Right foot only?" Carla asked.

"Yes. You never use your left foot to drive. Never. Do you understand?" I tried to be calm.

"Yes, Nancy. Right foot only." Carla tried to sound confident.

She seemed to understand, but with Carla, I was never sure. She put her right foot on the brake and put the car in reverse. She inched the car out of the driveway and onto the road. And then … jerk … we came to a stop. Both her left and right feet were on the brake.

"Right foot only," I said as I looked around to make sure we were not holding up traffic. Luckily, there were no other cars on the road.

"Yes, yes. Right foot," Carla said. She took her left foot off the brake, put the car into drive, and accelerated slowly down the road. We drove to the local elementary school, and I asked her to park, back up, and park again. Over and over. We drove around and around the school for about thirty minutes with me constantly reminding her "right foot, right foot, right foot." I chanted the mantra over and over again. After a while, she got it, slowly.

I came home, called a driving school, and arranged for lessons. I then poured myself a big glass of wine. That night, I went to bed, thinking, *Right foot. Right foot. Right foot.*

Review local traffic laws with your au pair and show her where she can park. Buy a state driver's manual and have her study it. Check with your state to see if your au pair can get a state driver's license. Studying for the test will help her learn local driving laws. It will also help to have a local license if she is ever stopped by the police.

Parking Matters

Even our male au pair, Bobby, who had a great deal of driving experience, had issues with the car. He never once had an accident, but boy, did he have trouble parking.

Bobby usually forgot to put money in the parking meter, or he would park the car illegally. Twice during his first month, Bobby went to the gym and got parking tickets. He would place the tickets on the pile of mail that had been delivered that day, and I would find them later. I paid the tickets but reminded him that he needed to feed the meter. He promised to try to remember. After paying the second parking ticket, I told him that I would not pay for any more. We put a huge pile of quarters in the car for him to use. That helped.

TIP: Stock the car with quarters and dimes for the parking meters.

Cleaning the Vehicle

Tell your au pair to keep the car clean. One day during the few short months when Lena was our au pair, my husband, Mark, walked in the house after a morning workout and stood directly in front of me.

"Come with me," he said. I knew something must be wrong with the car. Had she hit something? Dented the car without telling us? No. There, stuck on the dashboard right above the speedometer was a chewed-up wad of gum, sans wrapper. Just gum, glistening in the heat of the sun.

I shuddered. When Lena came downstairs that morning, Mark gave her a short, stern lecture about respecting our things, keeping the car clean, and absolutely never, ever, placing a wad of gum on the dashboard. A few days later, I got in the car, and something caught my eye. There was a silver gum wrapper around a wadded-up piece of Extra chewing gum lodged in the small space to the right of the wheel where the steering column goes deep into the car. I immediately summoned Lena. I asked her to get it out, but the harder she tried, the deeper the wad lodged into the steering wheel. To this day, I drive the car and see that silver-wrapped wad of gum mocking me.

Insurance Matters

Each state and each insurance carrier has its own policies regarding au pairs, so do your homework on the regulations in your home state and with your insurance carrier. Ask your au pair to bring her home country's driver's license, too. Your insurance carrier may want to see it. Your local coordinator will be able to tell you the guidelines for your home state.

If your au pair gets into a serious accident with your car, she is responsible for $250 toward the insurance deductible. This requirement is set by the State Department as part of the au pair policies.

Keep in mind that male au pairs are more expensive than female au pairs when it comes to adding them to your car insurance. Also, an older au pair will cost less to insure than a younger au pair.

Despite the risks of having your au pair drive your car, be generous with it. Don't penny-pinch over gas. Don't be neurotic about how many miles she is driving. In the beginning, be sure to evaluate her driving ability, but once you are comfortable that she is as proficient as every other driver on the road, let her go. Just be sure to put a GPS in the car; that way, she'll be sure to be able to find her way home.

Considering a Family Vacation with Your Au Pair

There will come a time during the year when you will plan a family vacation or you might have to go away for a weekend. Should you take your au pair on vacation? The answer depends on how much you like your au pair.

Clearly, there is significant expense incurred if you bring your au pair with you on vacation. You will have to buy an extra plane ticket and book a separate room for your au pair or have her share a room with your kids. You will pay for meals and activities for your au pair. Having along a built-in babysitter has its pros and cons.

According to the au pair program guidelines, travel with the host family is considered "on duty hours." So you will need to clarify in advance when she will be on and off duty and specify exactly what the au pair's responsibilities will be while on vacation. When is she supposed to wake up? When will she have time off? If this is a working vacation, tell her exactly when she will be working. If you don't clarify this, she will sleep until noon and laze by the pool all day while you are running around after your child.

Every year, I have a problem with my kids' spring break. Their school vacation falls on the third week of April, the same week I have an annual conference. What to do?

One year, my mom took the boys and Sally to Disney World. We were happy to pay for most of the trip, and they all had a blast. Will and Sally rode the roller coasters, and Hank and my mom rode the lazy river ride. Sally was easygoing, and she and my mom got along well.

One year, I brought the boys and Karen along with me to the conference. During the day, they swam in the hotel pool and horsed around the hotel room. At night, we went to dinner and the movies. Karen and I talked about her love life and drank wine. It was a good week.

TIP: If your au pair is going to be a drag, leave her at home and hire a babysitter at the hotel.

If your au pair is not a fabulous match and you don't really like spending loads of time with her, a vacation with your au pair can be dreadful. Think twice before booking that extra room. Vacations require a lot of togetherness. We learned that the hard way when we took Andrea with us on vacation to Sante Fe, New Mexico, to attend a family wedding. We brought Andrea with us so she could babysit the boys during the various wedding parties at the adobe resort in the heart of Sante Fe. This was about week five of Andrea's adjustment to being an au pair, and I already knew that she was miserable in New Jersey. I should have guessed that she would be miserable in Sante Fe, too.

We arrived and checked in to the hotel. Andrea had her own room, complete with a queen-sized bed made out of tree trunks, with flannel blankets and a terry-cloth robe and slippers. She had a mini-bar and a TV with about one hundred movie channels. We all walked to the center of Sante Fe for lunch and found a cute Tex-Mex diner in the town square. Andrea could not find anything on the menu that she wanted to eat. I tried to translate. She didn't understand. She looked at me with tears in her eyes. "I do not like Mexican food," she said. She ate french fries with Hank.

That night when Mark and I had to attend the rehearsal dinner, Andrea babysat the boys and watched them swim in the pool, wrapped up in her terry-cloth robe. She did not want to swim, she told me. The water was too cold.

The next day, before the wedding ceremony, we had time for some sightseeing. We decided to explore the local Native American cliff dwellings. Andrea met us in the lobby in her "work outfit": navy dress pants, white blouse, red sweater, and heels. This was not exactly the jeans and sneakers I had suggested. I asked her if she had a pair of sneakers.

"I forgot my sneakers," she replied, sullenly. "I will be fine." She kept up with us as we walked down dusty trails to get to the cliff dwellings. But she stayed at the bottom, sitting on a rock, when we climbed up the ladders and steep trails. "I am afraid," she said. And miserable, too. When we all came down and met her at the bottom, I could tell she had been crying again.

We checked out of the hotel on Sunday, and as I perused that bill, I saw $50 in extra charges from Andrea's room. She had eaten two cans of nuts, a package of Famous Amos cookies, and a bag of Doritos and had drunk an $8 bottle of water. The girl had drowned her sorrows in the mini-bar.

Be Specific about Rules of the Kitchen

I have normal, everyday kids. They are not exotic eaters. They eat "kid" food. Upon arrival, most au pairs have no clue what constitutes American "kid food." You have to be very clear. I found that I needed to literally list out each and every food that each child ate and then show each au pair what the packages look like. Manage your expectations: very few au pairs are good cooks.

 Kit was the most enthusiastic in the kitchen of all our au pairs. She wasn't a particularly good cook, and she always left the kitchen a complete mess. But she had the best of intentions. She arrived with a cookbook for kids and was eager to introduce the boys to New Zealand dishes. Unfortunately, every measurement was metric (and she wasn't very good at translating), and the ingredients were all but impossible to find (try finding Knorr brand dried celery soup mix at your grocery store!).

They muddled through, experimenting in the kitchen together and building their friendship. The cooking projects of choice were making potato wedges sprinkled with salt and paprika, and baking cookies from a box. Kit and Hank would make cookies several times per week. Hank would crack the eggs, pour the oil, turn on the mixer, and eat the batter. Kit would spoon out the dough on the cookie sheet and spoon-feed Hank the batter from the bowl. Together they would monitor the cooking progress through the window in the oven. Hank would eat the cookies warm. Kit would eat the cookies cold. It was a match made in heaven.

TIP: In the beginning, ask your au pair to watch you cook meals for your children for several days.

Be very specific about what your children will eat for meals. Write out the list of foods that your kids eat. Show your au pair how to cook these foods and where they are stored. Show her what to do with the leftovers. Leave the list in the kitchen.

Andrea lost any hope of connecting with the boys one night over dinner in what has become known in our house as "The Brazilian Food Incident."

One evening about three weeks after Andrea had arrived and three weeks before we rematched, I walked in the house, and there, at the kitchen table, were the boys and Andrea, staring at each other in a stalemate. I could feel the tension in the room. No one was saying a word. In front of each boy was a dinner plate piled high with what looked like pieces of chicken, slathered in a dark brown sauce, and chopped vegetables atop a pile of rice. The boys were slumped in their chairs. Their arms were crossed on their chests. Will glared at me as I walked in the room. Hank looked at me with teary eyes.

"What's up?" I asked, trying to sound cheerful but worried about what I was seeing. I admit it: Up until that moment, I had not exactly done the best job at exposing my kids to international cuisines. If we went out for Chinese food (which we didn't do very often), Hank might eat a few bites of rice. Will would eat rice and wonton soup. Their idea of exotic food was pizza. I know; it's sad. Their rules were simple: Meat and vegetables must never touch. Sauces are scary.

Asking my boys to eat a dish in which meat and vegetables were combined with a sauce would be the same thing as asking them to do calculus. Will is more adventurous than Hank.

He eats broccoli, string beans, and artichokes. He loves a good steak, lamb chops, and chicken wings. Hank is an entirely different story. Hank eats twelve things on the face of the earth. I had attempted to describe to Andrea the finer points of Hank's List of Approved Foods, but something had gotten lost in translation. Andrea had clearly not understood my list of suggested dinners. She had gone completely off the map. What she had served them was not chicken nuggets and fries, macaroni and cheese, baked potatoes, hot dogs, or noodles with butter. This was serious, sophisticated Brazilian food. I couldn't tell exactly what was in it, but I think I saw something that looked like a saucy red pepper poking out from underneath the chicken chunks.

"Will and Hank no eat their dinner," Andrea stated stubbornly and sat up tall in her chair. She had her arms crossed, too. "I told them they have to stay at the table 'til they eat."

Hank looked up at me. As soon as I made eye contact with him, his teary eyes burst, and he sobbed in his seat. He had been able to hold it together until he saw me, and now it was over. Forcing Hank to sit at the table in front of a plate of food that was not on The List was like asking a vegan to eat prime rib. He would sit at the table for a very long time, getting more and more upset. In the end, he would throw up.

A typical eldest child, Will respects authority and tried Andrea's dish. "I tried it, Mom! I did. Didn't I, Andrea?" Will yelled, slightly hysterical. "But it is spicy, and there are onions. And look, the onions have SAUCE on them." Will would not eat foods that were mixed. He would eat vegetables and meat but not if they were cooked together in the same pot. "But I TRIED IT, Mom. I tried it." He thought that this should be good enough. It would have been in my book. But now, Will was exasperated. "And now, SHE WILL NOT LET US BE EXCUSED!"

This was Andrea's dinner. She had chopped up green and red peppers, onions, and tomatoes and had fried them with oil, garlic, and spices. The whole thing went in the oven with cooked diced chicken to make a lovely casserole thing. I thought it was mouthwatering, and it smelled great. But this was not a dinner for my simple salt-and-pepper kids.

"Will and Hank," I told the boys, "you may be excused. Go ahead and play. I will get you something else to eat in a minute. Give me some time to talk to Andrea." I ushered them out of the room, giving Hank a kiss on the head and wiping his tears on his way out.

"Andrea," I began, "I appreciate that you cooked for the boys, and I'm sure that Mark and I will love to eat what you made. But this is not a dinner that Will and Hank will eat. Please look at the list of things that I have suggested. I know that they are not exciting or fun to cook, but these are the foods that the boys will eat."

"But chicken nuggets not healthy," she protested. "I cook good food. This better than chicken nuggets. This food better for them." I sensed a stubborn streak.

"I know that it is, and I am sure you cook well, Andrea," I replied, "but the boys only eat simple food. Please just cook them things that are on the list of foods that I gave you. Please."

She stood up and harrumphed up the stairs. I took a box of chicken nuggets and bag of fries out of the freezer and put them in the oven. I sat down, poured myself a glass of wine, and ate both plates of Andrea's meal. It was delicious.

Dinner Time

Food, feeding, cooking, and meal preparation can develop into a real issue with your au pair. Sabrina drove me crazy around dinnertime. Typically, I would get home around 5:30 p.m. and would prepare dinner for the kids. I really enjoyed sitting with them and eating dinner. It was a great opportunity to catch up on their day. So on a normal day, dinner preparation was not part of Sabrina's duties. But if I was going to be late, she was responsible for getting them something to eat. The problem was she could just never, ever remember this.

> *Maintain a regular dinnertime and make sure that the au pair knows that if you are not around to cook, she must do it.*

One particular day, I got home around 7:30 p.m. and walked into the house to hear the boys screaming their heads off at each other. LEGOs were being hurled at heads. Nerf bullets were flying through the air. Sabrina sat at the kitchen table, feebly trying to calm them down.

"What's going on?" I asked. "Will! Hank! Stop it!" I shouted. They paused the barrage, and I asked them to sit at the kitchen table. In one instant, I knew exactly what the problem was.

"Have you eaten dinner?" I asked.

They looked at me with big eyes. Sabrina looked at me with big eyes. It was a typical "aha!" moment.

"I forgot," Sabrina said, anticipating my question. Forgot? Why is it that a mother can diagnose the problem in a split second and an au pair will live through an hour of bickering and not once ask herself "Why?"

Food Builds Relationships
I do recognize that food can bring us together. It can be a wonderful moment of connection between an au pair and her kids. Take Hank, for example. As you now know, he is one of the pickiest eaters ever (even my mother says so). At the age of ten, he still has a gag reflex so strong that if you force him to eat something, you will soon be wearing it. He will puke up anything that is not on Hank's List of Approved Foods. But for each au pair, he has carefully added one food to the list. He somehow associates that one food with the au pair. But when she goes, so, too, does the food. It gets dropped from the list.

For Vera, Hank ate bacon. He ate exactly two slices of crispy, almost-burnt bacon for breakfast, lunch, and dinner almost every day that Vera was with us. And when she moved out, so did the bacon. Hank rarely eats it. Bacon is off the list.

TIP: Allow your au pair to have a special food with your child. This is a way to encourage that au pair–child connection.

Hank and Kit developed a close relationship based completely on chocolate. Hank loves chocolate. Kit loved chocolate. For an entire year, Kit persuaded Hank to go to school by leading him to the front door with a pocketful of M&Ms, which she would slowly dole out during their walk to school. To this day, he will look at me before leaving the house and, with a big smile, ask, "Treat for the road?" as he heads for the candy dish in the living room en route to the front door. Chocolate has stayed on The List.

For Bobby, Hank ate English muffins. Hank preferred them toasted to a dark, dark brown. Not black and not golden—dDark brown right before it burns. Making the perfect English muffin for Hank required serious monitoring of the toaster, but Bobby was tall, and it was easy for him to see inside the toaster and pop it up at the perfect browness.

For Sabrina, Hank ate homemade waffles. She would make the batter and pour the mix onto the waffle iron. When the waffle had been cooked to perfection, Hank carefully instructed Sabrina to put the butter on the side, because if she buttered the waffle, it would soon get too soggy (gross!).

TIP: Use food to get to know your au pair. Ask your au pair to share a typical meal from her country. But don't force your kids to eat it!

Over the years and au pairs, Will has acquired several cooking specialties. From KiKi, he learned to make sushi. KiKi made Japanese cooking both a science experiment and an art project. She never forced the boys to eat what they made in the kitchen. Soon, Will was boasting that when he grew up, he would go to Japan and be the only blonde sushi chef in the country. He wasn't eating very much sushi, but he was making it and proudly showing off every creation. One day, Will and KiKi created a platter of homemade sushi, and he took it in to school as his "show-and-tell." KiKi had been a sushi chef back home and was happy to show the boys how to make proper Japanese sushi rolls.

At first, KiKi taught Will to make simple California rolls with cucumber and avocado. Then they graduated to fish sushi rolls and sushi rolls "inside out" (with the rice on the outside). When KiKi was cooking for herself, she would put anything on a sushi roll: fried eggs; green, red, or yellow peppers; asparagus; tomatoes; even ham or turkey. She would put a little mayonnaise on the nori before rolling the sushi. My personal favorite was mayonnaise, hot dog, and scrambled egg sushi.

Karen from South Africa was our only au pair who made any significant progress getting Hank to eat new foods. During her seven months with us, Hank tried celery and edamame beans. I can't say that these foods became a staple in Hank's diet, but he did try them and ate them on more than one occasion. It was a victory, small but significant. Of course, then Karen left, and Hank hasn't looked at a celery stalk since.

Dining Habits

I have a confession about my family. We do not sit down and have a family meal every night. I know that the studies tell me that sitting down together is the thing to do, but I just cannot get organized to make a big meal every night. Besides, my boys are hungry way before Mark gets home from work, and I eat out often, having fancy lunches in nice NYC restaurants, leaving me no appetite for dinner. I am sure to tell my au pairs about our dining patterns in the interview process, but nevertheless, this has proven to be a disappointment to some of my au pairs.

> *TIP: In the interview process, tell your au pair about your family's daily dining habits, especially if she will be responsible for cooking her own meals.*

Many nights, we will sit down together, but it will likely be with takeout. Or we will all just grab something easy—a sandwich, a salad (in Will's case, a cheeseburger; in Hank's case, a waffle)—and sit together watching a Yankees game. Sunday nights are our family dinner night, usually with a family game afterward. I encourage our au pairs to be home for Sunday-night dinners.

Unfortunately for Bobby, his expectation of American family life included the daily meat-and-potato family dinner. He arrived as our au pair having never really cooked for himself. Responsible for his own dinner most nights, Bobby became a pasta-maker extraordinaire. He mastered the boiling of water, the cooking of pasta (boxes and boxes of it), the heating of sauce (jars and jars of it), and the shaking of parmesan cheese. Occasionally, Bobby would make a turkey burger or a big sandwich—on potato bread, of course.

> *TIP: Family meals will help au pairs feel included. This is an important part of the cultural exchange that builds family connections. So make a point of including your au pair in at least one family dinner per week.*

When my parents came to visit, Bobby was in heaven. On these occasions, my dad cooked up a double recipe of whatever he made so we would have leftovers for the week. On one occasion, my dad made a huge veal parmesan, and we enjoyed a wonderful family dinner complete with several loaves of his homemade French bread, wine, and good conversation. Bobby devoured the dinner. He went back for seconds and hung around the table for a nice evening of cultural exchange.

When I got home from work the next day, the week's worth of leftovers were gone. All of them. My dad had been hanging around the house that day and ate lunch with Bobby. Together, they had finished the veal parmesan. Over their meal together, Bobby had looked seriously at my father and said, sounding just like Arnold Schwarzenegger, "You should visit more often."

Teach Your Au Pair How to Use Your Appliances

In the Kitchen
One of the biggest adjustments that your au pair will make is learning how to use the appliances in your kitchen. Our big refrigerators (especially the ones with the ice and water dispensers in the doors) are intimidating. Our dishwashers are foreign. Garbage disposals are downright scary. Like the rest of our culture, our kitchens are super-sized. It takes a while for au pairs to get used to them.

Think about it: We live most of our lives in our kitchens, which is very unlike most other cultures. Here in America, our kitchen is our living room, our study hall, our dining room, and our home office.

Your au pair will not be accustomed to buying in bulk from Costco and storing food in huge refrigerators or freezers in your basement. Most au pairs will not know the definitions for Tupperware, "baggies," or even "leftovers."

Prepare yourself for spending a lot of time showing your au pair how to use your kitchen. Do not assume that she knows how to use the stove, the oven, or even the microwave. Show your au pair where the pots and pans are and describe the way you like them cleaned. You will need to show your au pair how to load the dishwasher and where you keep the dishwasher soap. Be sure to describe the difference between dishwashing soap for the sink and dishwashing soap for the dishwasher. I have had more than one kitchen flood for the misunderstanding.

You will also need to show your au pair what foods need to be refrigerated and how you prefer to store uneaten food. Show her where you keep plastic containers and plastic bags for food storage.

I have lost much food because my au pair didn't know where it should go after being used. One day while Karen was our au pair, I was unpacking the groceries and trying to make room in the cupboard. There, I found several jars of half-eaten pasta sauce (one with a significant amount of mold on it) sitting on the shelf. I reminded Karen that opened jars of sauce needed to be refrigerated. She told me that in South Africa, the jars were not so big, so they rarely had leftovers. She had found the sauce in the cupboard and figured that was where she should put it after she had used some of it.

Write out the instructions for where the garbage goes and where to find extra garbage bags. Just like anyone else, au pairs hate to take out the garbage.

In the Laundry
You can absolutely have your au pair do your kids' laundry. Unfortunately, you cannot ask your au pair to do your laundry. But would you want to? Picture your au pair folding your spouse's undies. No thank you!

Like the appliances in your kitchen, your au pair is likely to be new to the size and structure of the washer and convenience of the clothes dryer, especially the super-capacity types. None of my au pairs had ever used a clothes dryer before arriving in my house. It is also very likely that your au pair's mother always did her laundry for her. You must teach her everything: how to sort the clothes, how big a load should be, how to load and unload the laundry, how much detergent to use, if and when you use bleach or fabric softener, what should line dry and what can go in the dryer, and how to fold the laundry.

Type out the instructions for how to use your washer and dryer and post them in your laundry room. Show your au pair where you keep your laundry detergent. In the beginning, hide the bleach. And of course, be sure to tell your au pair the most important rule of laundry: Never, ever put a brand-new red sweatshirt in with the whites. All of my boys' white briefs and socks were pink after Bobby did a load of their laundry.

Once my au pairs have mastered the basics of washing and drying the clothes, the folding and putting-away has always remained a challenge. Sabrina, for example, always folded the clothes and put them away inside out. Forgive him, but at twelve years old, Hank did not look carefully before he put on a shirt. More than a dozen times, I found myself telling him to turn his shirt right-side-out at the breakfast table.

Like most boys, my kids are brutal on their clothes: holes in the knees of pants, rips in the sides of shirts, and grass stains galore. (Is it just me, or are they just not making clothes the way they used to?) Anyway, each of my au pairs was always oblivious to the disreputable state of the boys' clothes. They would wash them, fold them, and put them away in their drawers, in their horrible state ... only to live for another day. This drove me crazy, until I finally placed a special basket in the laundry room and labeled it: "clothes to be repaired." Then, the au pairs would pile the clothes (yes, inside out) in the basket, and when the basket was full, I would survey the damage, throw out what could not be saved, and mend the rest.

TIP: Create a space in your laundry room where your au pair can put clothes that are torn, stained, or damaged. You can then take a look and decide for yourself to repair or throw them out.

Expect Others to Take an Interest in Your Au Pair

Regardless of where you live, you should know that your friends, your family, your neighbors, and people you hardly know will take a special interest in your au pair.

When Bobby's modeling career took off, every mom on the playground wanted to help. Bobby was the talk of Hank's school community. At drop-off and pickup, Bobby was surrounded by moms arranging playdates and asking how the career was going. Every mom in town wanted to know who the great-looking guy was walking Hank to school every day. I was stopped on the train platform, on the sidewalk, in the grocery store. "Who is your new babysitter?" I was asked, repeatedly. I had frightening visions of the local Mrs. Robinson attempting to seduce my au pair!

I only made the occasional appearance on the playground to pick up Hank, but I was told that moms who had previously worn sweatpants and baseball caps to school for drop-off were suddenly dressing up and wearing makeup. They were seeking Bobby out to arrange playdates and offer whatever help he needed so he could pursue his modeling career. Soon, Bobby had the phone numbers of all the moms in town programmed into his phone. If he missed the train home from NYC, he would call "David's mom" or "Kevin's mom" to ask if Hank could have a playdate. They were overjoyed to help.

When you welcome an au pair into your immediate family, she is joining your extended family, too. It is likely that your family and friends will immediately form attachments and share their opinions. My father became very fond of our first au pair, Vera. After her year with us was complete, he actually sponsored her visa to stay in this country and become a full-time student. Her schedule as a full-time student did not allow her to stay on as our au pair, but my dad and Vera stayed in touch. On each trip, my dad delivered home-baked bread to our former au pair.

KiKi and my mother bonded during one school vacation when they witnessed a carjacking. It was during a long weekend when the kids were off and I had to work. I had sent KiKi and the kids to visit my mom and dad in Maryland. While they were there, KiKi had arranged to see a family friend who lived outside of Baltimore.

They had arranged to rendezvous at a mall off a major highway that was easy for everyone to find. KiKi and my mom had carefully printed the MapQuest directions to the mall and confidently headed out. (All au pairs are really good at MapQuest. They must go over this in the orientation.) Applebee's was the designated meeting place. KiKi, my mom, and my boys arrived early at the shopping center, parked, and walked around, waiting for KiKi's friend. Will used the opportunity to call me in the office to tell me that absolutely nothing was going on—which is a fairly typical call from a ten-year-old who has just mastered using a cell phone.

As we were talking about absolutely nothing, I could tell that something else was happening in the background. KiKi's friend had arrived. There was a commotion and then I heard:

"WAIT!"

"STOP!"

"MY CAR!"

"STOP!"

After that, I heard a whole bunch of screaming.

"Will!" I yelled. Was he even on the phone any more? I couldn't tell. "Will! What is happening? Are you OK?"

"Mom!" Will yelled into the phone. "The car. Mom! A guy! He jumped in the car and took off!" Will was hyperventilating, he was so excited. "Mom. He STOLE KiKi's friend's CAR!" This was the highlight of the vacation, maybe his life.

KiKi's friend had stopped her car and hopped out to give KiKi a hug, leaving the car running in the road with the driver's door wide open. As she was chatting and being introduced to the family, a young man had run up, jumped into the driver's seat, slammed the door, put the car in drive, and torn out of the parking lot. KiKi, her friend, my mom, Will, and Hank had been left standing, in shock, on the sidewalk outside of Applebee's.

They spent the rest of the afternoon eating lunch at Applebee's and giving statements to the police. They were each interviewed and asked to give their version of events and a description of the thief to the detective. The boys (and my mother) thought it was all very exciting.

The experience of witnessing the crime bonded KiKi and my mother. They were best buddies after the carjacking.

Overlap Your Au Pairs

Once you have had a few au pairs, you will find that one of the most time-consuming (and often tedious) parts of getting a new au pair is the first few weeks of au pair training. So what I have figured out is that the best way to do it is to have your old au pair train the new au pair. This works best, however, when you like the au pair who is leaving.

Having your au pairs overlap has positives and negatives. Your old au pair will help with training the new au pair. She will introduce her to the au pairs in the area, drive her around town, and show her the ropes. The transition will be smoother for the children. Your old au pair's bad habits might rub off on the new au pair, however, and the old au pair will most definitely tell your new au pair all your family secrets.

When we matched with Bobby, we asked if KiKi would help with the transition before heading home to Japan. She was happy to do so. The plan was that KiKi would help Bobby learn about our family, and the kids would have a smooth transition.

Right away, Bobby and KiKi started sharing interests and experiences. They were both interested in fashion. They both were enthralled by New York City. Throughout the first week, KiKi showed Bobby how to pack lunches, unpack backpacks, and help the boys with their homework. She introduced Bobby to all the moms on the playground at the school. She showed him around our town and, most importantly, how to get in and out of New York City and still be at school at 3:00 p.m. to pick up the boys. KiKi introduced Bobby to all of her fashion friends in New York City, and from person after person, he heard, "Are you a model?" or "You should model." A seed was planted.

After we matched with Carla, we asked Sally to stick around and overlap for about a week before returning to Germany. Sally showed Carla the routine, helped the boys get to know her, drove her around town, and introduced her to some of the au pairs in town. Sally even organized a dinner party to introduce Carla to her friends who would still be in the area.

Sally and I enthusiastically planned the farewell party for Sally, which would also be a "coming out" party for Carla. Sally invited every au pair that she knew. I made a great chicken barbeque in a Crock-Pot that the girls piled on soft rolls and devoured. We had plenty of beer and iced tea on hand. Ten girls—from Germany, Norway, Sweden, Austria, and Brazil—sat on the back porch and chatted. Sally introduced Carla to everyone, and they all settled in to get to know each other. Carla sat on the edge of the group, and as soon as she finished her dinner, she quickly got up and left. She disappeared upstairs and did not come back down for the rest of the evening. At one point, Sally went upstairs to encourage Carla to come back down but could not convince her. Sally kicked back, drank another beer, and didn't worry any more about it. She and her friends had a wonderful time.

Before Sally left us, I asked her what she thought of Carla. I valued Sally's opinion and knew she would tell me the truth.

"Well, Nancy," Sally told me gently, "I've noticed a few things: Carla is a terrible driver. She is very timid with the boys. She doesn't want to have any other kind of friends except Korean friends, which means she is going to have a terrible time learning English. She doesn't like American food. Oh, and she really doesn't like Ginger. She is just not a dog person."

Wow. Sally had nailed it. Forever an optimist, she added, "But she is super nice! Give her some time. It might work out." My heart sank.

Don't Leave an Au Pair Overnight with Your Kids

The State Department regulations prohibit an au pair from staying with your children overnight alone. I know of plenty of host parents who have asked their au pair to do overnight babysitting, but let me clarify the rule: It's a no-no.

In our house, if Mark and I plan to go away together for a few nights, I always ask my mom and dad to come and do the "overnight" babysitting. Before getting on that plane, however, I make sure that everyone is clear about their responsibilities.

If you are leaving your au pair with grandparents or others who are doing overnight babysitting, be sure to clarify when your au pair will be on duty or off duty, especially if the schedule represents a change from the norm. Share the schedule with the overnight babysitters so they will know what to expect from the au pair. Write out a schedule for your time away and post it where everyone can see it.

Last year, I tagged along on a trip that Mark took to Hong Kong, and my mom and dad were generous enough to come and stay with Sabrina and our boys. My parents had done this before and always looked forward to getting to know our au pair and spending some quality time with their grandchildren. My dad would spend the days baking bread and reading books. My mom would take on a special house project for me (cleaning my refrigerator was always welcome). They would make dinner every night and linger over the dinner table, often talking with our au pairs for long periods before putting the boys to bed. I was sure this trip would be an easy assignment. I was wrong.

When I got home, my mom and dad were exhausted and quickly made their exit back home to Maryland. My mother reported that at 5:30 p.m. every night, Sabrina had announced that she was "off duty" and disappeared to her room or left the house to go to the gym. She had left my mother to get the kids dinner and put them to bed, drive them to scout meetings, and even one harrowing evening, drive through a rainstorm to Will's rock-climbing lesson. Sabrina had not once stuck around to have dinner with them.

I was furious at Sabrina for taking advantage of my parents but also realized that perhaps I had not been clear enough with her about what my expectations would be: to help out and especially to do the evening driving for my seventy-something-year-old mother. My mother was too much of a softy to ask Sabrina to pitch in. But my mother never liked Sabrina after that.

Lay Down the Rules of Discipline

In the very beginning, you must speak to your au pair about your philosophy of parenting and how you expect her to discipline your children. Do you use a "three strikes" rule? A "time out" rule? A "take away privileges" rule? You must decide and stick with it.

You must tell your children that your au pair is in charge, and they must know that the au pair has the authority to discipline them if they are out of line. Your au pair must have the authority and the confidence to effectively discipline your children, or they will walk all over her.

Once your children know that the au pair is in charge and will discipline them, you must tell your au pair exactly what she can and can't do for discipline. A quick slap or spanking might be perfectly acceptable where your au pair is from, so if that thought frightens you, be very clear that spanking is not the way you discipline your children.

In our house, we use "time outs" that have become "go to your room!" We've found that separating the children when they are fighting is the most effective way to resolve conflict. What doesn't work is when the kids pick up the phone and call me at work.

From day one, we tell our au pair to be firm with the kids and discipline them when needed. And we ask her to avoid, at all costs, the dreaded call to Mommy.

CHAPTER 4:

A HAPPY AU PAIR MAKES FOR A HAPPY FAMILY

If my au pair is happy, my children are happy. And if my children are happy, I will be happy. So I have decided that it is in my own best interest to do whatever I can to make my au pair happy. I don't cater to her every whim, but I have learned a few things over the years that help my au pair know that she is appreciated and even loved.

Make Your Au Pair's Room Her Castle

An important part of making your au pair happy is to create a room for her that is comfortable, private, and personalized. This does not have to cost a lot of money. I now make a trip to Target a regular stop on my tour of our town, and ask my new au pair to pick out a few things for her room. It can be a new poster, a pillow, an area rug, or a new duvet cover. I discourage candles—too dangerous.

TIP: Make your au pair's room private and personalized. Take her to a home goods store and let her pick out some pillows, pictures, or a throw rug for her room.

Vera had lived in a Soviet-style cinder-block apartment and shared a bedroom with her brother. The third-floor au pair suite was the most space she had ever had to herself. She loved the cable TV and the large bookshelves stocked with novels.

Kit had grown up in a one-story ranch house on a sheep farm with exactly five steps leading to the front door. She had shared a bathroom with three sisters, her mother, and her father. She had never slept in a room by herself before. She was thrilled to have our third-floor au pair suite all to herself, but getting up there was a challenge. That many flights of stairs just about killed her. On her first day, she just about collapsed at the kitchen table, winded from climbing down all the stairs in our house. She was a heavy walker, too. We soon got used to it. Every morning, Kit would gallop down the back stairs with a rumble and harrumph into a chair at the kitchen table, already exhausted. There was something about Kit, however; she always had a smile on her face.

Sabrina from Germany told us that the apartment she had shared with her mother rarely had heat in the winter, so she was used to sleeping under five or six blankets. It was a bit of an adjustment for her to live in our attic, to which all the heat rose.

Karen from South Africa had lived in a house that had bars on every window because of the high crime rate in that country. She was amazed to learn that although we have an alarm on our house, we rarely set it.

Most au pairs come to the United States from fairly modest backgrounds in their home countries, so living in a typical American house is like living in a castle. Not having to share a bathroom, having wireless Internet access, and, in some cases, having a bed all to herself is the best part of the cultural exchange.

Force Your Au Pair to Go to Cluster Events (She Will Make Friends)

As part of the State Department regulations, the au pair agencies are required to provide regular social events for the au pairs. The purpose of these gatherings is to provide a support network for the au pairs and to prevent them from becoming depressed, suicidal, or worse (remember Louise Woodward?). Going to cluster events brings them together and forces them to make friends, which can be hard for new au pairs, especially if they do not speak English well.

Some of our au pairs have gladly gone to cluster events, and others have been reluctant. You should make attendance at cluster events mandatory for your au pair for at least the first six months of her year with you. Discuss this expectation with her as soon as she arrives.

Vera did not attend a cluster event for the first six months that she lived with us. This distressed the coordinator and me, and finally, we forced her to go to a cluster meeting. I told her that attendance at the cluster event was mandatory, and if she did not attend, she would risk not getting her $500 completion bonus (an au pair incentive that no longer exists). Bingo! That got her attention. The threat worked. Vera went to the next cluster event organized by the coordinator—rock climbing at a local gym. Much to my delight, Vera fell in love with the sport and came home smiling. We hadn't seen too much smiling up until that point, so I seized the opportunity. I offered to pay for a three-month membership to the climbing gym. The next day, we signed her up. I was willing to do anything to get her out of the house more often.

Climbing at the gym changed Vera's life and her disposition. She was slightly less severe at home, and we saw an occasional smile. She was still closely guarded about any and all details of her life, but she seemed to relax. I soon learned that Vera had a boyfriend named Greg. She had met him at the rock gym. Today, they are married.

Sally had the best social life of any of our au pairs. She quickly made friends with au pairs from Germany, Sweden, Norway, and Austria. There is a minor drawback to these relationships, because when au pairs get together, they all like to compare their host families' quirks and perks. Besides Justin Timberlake, cheap phone cards, MySpace, and travel, comparing host families is their favorite topic of conversation. Who is really working more than forty-five hours per week? Who is getting their gym membership paid for? Will the host family pay for all the gas in the car, or does the au pair have to pay for her own gas? Who has a GPS device in their car? Do host families lavish their au pairs with gifts? Do the host parents fight? Do the kids wet their beds? Do the au pairs go on exciting family vacations? Who is getting a divorce? Etc. Etc. Etc.

Don't Set a Curfew

Should you set a curfew for your au pair? My answer is no. Regardless of how old the au pair is, I believe that she should be treated as an adult. I tell my au pair after she arrives that I will treat her as an adult and expect that she will make responsible decisions in return. This includes making choices so that she can begin work every day on time and prepared to do her job. I remind her that there is no drinking and driving ever. We tell her that she is not allowed even one drink before she drives. Most au pairs have lived up to this agreement. During Au Pair Academy, this message is also drilled into the au pairs. During orientation with the local coordinator, they are again reminded to never, ever drink and drive.

Sally would go out several times per week, come home late, and still be ready to work and happy in the morning. From the first days in our house, she made friends with other au pairs. They were a stunning group going out at night—tall, blonde, beautiful young women. They would take turns driving, and they quickly had their social routine down pat. On Monday nights, they went to Starbucks. On Tuesday nights, they went to someone's house to watch *Gilmore Girls*. Wednesday was dance-lesson night at Diva Lounge, a local nightclub. Thursday was karaoke night at a local pub, where once a father from Hank's soccer team asked Sally for her number. She of course knew who he was and told him "No way!" The girls would go out at about seven, and even without a curfew, Sally would be home promptly at eleven. Of course, maybe her au pair friends had curfews and that is why she was always so punctual.

If she wanted to drink, Sally would walk the two miles to the next town, where the bars were. Or she would take a bus. Or have a friend drive. Sally loved to party but knew where and when to have fun, and then how to get home safely.

> *TIP: Have a no-tolerance policy for rules regarding drinking. If they are broken, have strict consequences.*

Lena was not so responsible. She was with us for about eight weeks one summer before we fired her and rematched. Lena would go out every night of the week. When I would inquire about what she was doing to keep so busy, she was very vague. She talked about a Czech boy who had come as an au pair and then stayed in the States illegally and was now living with and caring for an elderly man. He would call the house frequently, and the one time I met him, he gave me the creeps.

I reminded her about the no drinking and driving rule. I reminded her that I trusted her to be responsible while "on duty."

She must have forgotten. One lazy day in late August when the day camps were over and I was just dying for school to start again, I confronted something that I had never, in many years of having an au pair, dealt with. I was scheduled to leave that morning at my usual time: 7:00 a.m. Minutes before I had to leave the house, Lena came stumbling downstairs. I noticed more than the usual morning fog: greasy hair and crumpled pajamas, and she would not make eye contact with me. She slumped into the chair at the kitchen table, and I saw that her hands were shaking. The shakes? Did Lena have the shakes? What time had she gotten home? I hadn't heard her come in. She assured me in her gravelly voice that she was fine. I quickly put it out of my mind. I went to work.

Knowing that there was not anything formally scheduled for the day, I had suggested that she take the boys to the pool and then to the park to roller blade or ride bikes and scooters. I gave her $10 for all of them to get ice cream. But when I got home that evening, I noticed that the kids were still in the clothes that they had slept in. The $10 bill was still on the kitchen counter where I had left it that morning. Will told me that they had spent the entire day inside. He then told me that Lena had been asleep for the majority of the day on the couch in the basement.

My responsible elder child reported in great detail the events of the day: He had gotten Hank and himself breakfast. He had had Lucky Charms, and Hank had had a cereal bar. They had played LEGOs in the morning and then played on the computer. At lunch, Lena had made them an exceedingly nutritious lunch of popcorn, and they had watched the movie *xXx,* starring Vin Diesel. For those of you who don't know this cinematic masterpiece, *xXx* is rated PG-13 and has quite a bit of nudity, sex, violence, and bad language. To me, this movie was not even a little bit appropriate for my ten-year-old. It was definitely not appropriate for my seven-year-old. I was furious.

I asked Lena what had happened. She told me that the kids had complained that it was too hot outside and that they wanted to play inside in the air conditioning. She said that she could not get them to leave the house. She explained that she wanted to watch x*Xx* with the boys because it is partially set in Prague, near her hometown, and she thought it would be fun to show the boys her country. I asked her if she had thought at all about the rating of the movie. Did she think it would be appropriate for the boys? No, she said. She didn't know anything about movie ratings.

As soon as we fired Lena, I quickly revised the au pair handbook to include a description of the American system of movie ratings.

Invite Friends and Family to Stay

One way to truly integrate your au pair into your family is to invite her family to come for a visit. Not for weeks at a time, of course, but for a week or so. We have had several memorable au pair family visits.

TIP: Welcome family and friends of your au pair into your home. It will improve the cultural exchange.

Our first visitors were friends and family of KiKi. The word was out in Japan that she had settled into a great life in New York (well, near New York). Her friends and family started to arrive for a series of visits. First to visit was Nobu, her future fashion business partner, who was eager to make connections with people in the fashion world in New York. Nobu would go off to the city every day and explore. KiKi would meet her there in the evening, and they would have dinner and come home.

Then KiKi's boyfriend visited. His name was KJ, which stood for something that we could not pronounce. He did not speak one word of English, but in Japanese, he announced to KiKi that she had significantly changed since she'd left Japan. She promptly and confidently dumped him. That good-bye was a tad bit awkward. She couldn't wait for him to leave.

Next to visit was KiKi's brother Kazuki. Kazuki's English was a bit better than KJ's. He spoke about five words, including "rock and roll," "ice cream," "New York City," "party," and "crazy." He said "crazy!" a lot. Kazuki was a DJ in Japan and was in university. The boys thought he was a riot. In spite of the language differences, he settled right in with Will and Hank. They played touch football in the backyard and Nintendo in the basement. I learned that video games are a universal language. If you can play, you can communicate. You can shoot animated characters and build bridges.

According to KiKi, Kazuki was a typical Japanese teenager, but a little bit crazier. He wore baggy clothes, kept his hair longish and spiky, and sported a very uneven amount of facial hair (I couldn't tell if that was intentional or a consequence of being a nineteen-year-old boy). Regardless, Will and Hank thought Kazuki was cool and called him "Crazy Kazuki."

One day, Kazuki crossed the "crazy" line. It was a late afternoon, and when Hank got home from a playdate, KiKi asked him to eat a yogurt. Drinkable yogurts, brand name Danimals, were once on Hank's List of Approved Foods. That day, Hank was grousing about drinking his yogurt. Though not actually understanding the conversation between KiKi and Hank, Kazuki could tell what was going on. With the best of intentions, he leaned over, picked up the Danimal, and dramatically drank some of it to prove to Hank just how good drinkable yogurts could be. With a big sweeping gesture, Kazuki placed the yogurt down in front of Hank and sat back, smiling with a big yogurt mustache. Hank looked at Kazuki in horror, seeing the yogurt settling in to all of Kazuki's uneven whiskers. Scarred for life, Hank has never had a Danimal since.

TIP: Even invite the boyfriend.

Sally had a boyfriend named Andy. Six months into Sally's year in the U.S., Andy came for a visit. He was not at all what we had expected. He was different from the other young German guy we knew—Bobby, the male model. Andy was just as tall as Sally, and he was pale, with dark brown hair. When we met Andy, it was his hair that got our attention. Andy had dreadlocks down to his waist tied back with a scarf; he was a German Rastafarian. Andy's English was only so-so, but he had a voice that was deep and smooth. If his English had been better, I would have encouraged him to do voiceovers. Will and Hank got a kick out of him. They played video games and threw the football around in the backyard.

The Andy-and-Sally relationship puzzled us. Sally was a cigarette-smoking, junk food junkie, eating a diet that rivaled Hank's List of Approved Foods. Andy was a vegetarian and health conscious. What they did share was a laid-back personality. They were both easygoing and mellow. When they went to a restaurant, they would order one entrée. Sally would eat the meat. Andy would eat the vegetables. They would share the potatoes. According to Sally, this saved them tons of money.

While interviewing the au pair, let her know if you are open to having houseguests and how long they are welcome to stay. Have your au pair make plans in advance and try to coincide friend and family visits with your family vacation.

Banking and the Au Pair

The au pair stipend is tied directly to the federal minimum wage. The stipend is based on a U.S. Department of Labor calculation that takes the minimum wage for forty-five hours of work and then subtracts 40 percent for room and board. So it is no secret that au pairs do not make a lot of money; $195.75 per week is just not going to create an au pair millionaire.

Never mind that the pay is low; you will still need to get your au pair a bank account. You don't want her hanging around with too much cash, and she doesn't want the cash, either. She will just spend it.

Many au pairs come to the United States with the intention of saving as much as possible and taking home a nest egg at the end of their year. A few au pairs will send money home to their families to help with their expenses. Others are here to shop. After all, an Apple computer and a pair of Converse sneakers are much less expensive here than anywhere else in the world.

Be sure to make it clear with your au pair when payday is. Determine this in advance and stick to a system, whether you pay her weekly or monthly, in cash or by check. Many au pairs will ask for advances on their pay. Decide whether this is something you would be comfortable with.

Sabrina was by far the most obsessed with her payday. Several times throughout the six months that she was with us, she asked me if she could be paid in advance. She was constantly buying things on eBay and at the mall. She bought a Mac laptop while in the States. She was a serious shopper.

Bobby was frugal and spent his money well. Before he went home, he bought the latest iPod and a new digital camera.

Vera saved almost every dime. She was planning to pay for college in her au pair afterlife and needed every dime.

Kit spent her money on clothing and travel. She went to California and the Grand Canyon with her savings. She left without a dime.

Make sure that your au pair has an ATM card that is a "check card," which will allow her to make purchases online. All au pairs love eBay. With their own check cards, they will not ask you to use your PayPal account.

TIP: Set up direct deposit for your au pair.

I set up my au pair's bank account at my bank with direct deposit. Every Friday, an automatic deposit for her weekly salary goes into her account from mine. With this arrangement, I never have to worry about leaving her a check or cash. And I don't have to remind myself to pay her each week.

Get Creative with the Educational Requirement

As a host family, it is your responsibility to provide $500 toward the au pair's requirement to take college courses. The State Department regulation states that each au pair must take six credits, or sixty hours, of college-level courses during her year in the United States. The university or college where the au pair takes classes must be an accredited institution of higher learning, not an adult school, not a bartending school, not a for-profit English language school.

Taking classes is part of the cultural exchange. It is also a great way for your au pair to meet other young people and build a network of friends. It gives her structure in her free time and provides specific goals to work toward. As a host parent, you should work hard to get your au pair into good classes that she enjoys.

TIP: College courses during the day are usually attended by college-age students. Evening classes are attended by professionals. Sign up your au pair for classes in which she can meet people her own age.

Unfortunately for us host parents, it is very difficult to find any accredited college where $500 can get you sixty hours of classroom time. You will find the most cost-effective classes at your local community college.

Several colleges have developed special weekend courses just for au pairs. In these programs, the au pair arrives Friday afternoon and studies through Sunday afternoon, usually staying in a local motel. Each weekend is devoted to one particular theme, such as American history, American holidays, storytelling, or the history of American dance (to name a few). These weekend programs may require your au pair to do some reading and/or to write a paper in advance, but in one weekend, she will get thirty hours of coursework completed. The downside of these programs is that the au pairs come from various locations, so it is not a way for the au pair to build a group of friends. In addition, one weekend course is about $500, so you will blow your whole wad on exactly one-half of the requirement.

For more information about these weekend programs in the New York area, look at the CW Post campus of Long Island University, the College of St. Rose in the Adirondacks, and Manhattanville College. Ask the agency's local coordinator for information about similar programs in your area.

TIP: Do not sign your au pair up for classes the day after she arrives. If you rematch, you have lost those fees and must start over with your new au pair. Wait at least a month.

Auditing classes at the local college may be an option for your au pair. The State Department will accept audited classes for the requirement. However, my experience is that the fees associated with auditing are just as much as enrolling in the class, and the professor will pay more attention to your au pair as an enrolled student.

Before your first au pair arrives, explore the options at local colleges and universities in your community. Scour Web sites, looking for "continuing education" departments and "non-credit courses." These classes are best suited for your au pair. Prepare to invest some of your own time in finding this information for your au pair, because it is usually buried on the college Web sites.

Colleges and universities in big cities will often have interesting one-day, non-credit history and culture tours as part of their continuing education programs. For example, the Fashion Institute of Technology (FIT) in NYC offers guided tours of the city for less than $100. For about six hours, your au pair could explore the culture, history, and cuisine of SoHo and Little Italy with a hip professor and group of cool students. I'd like to sign up for that one!

Be generous with the educational requirement. Do what you can to make sure that your au pair is taking the classes that she wants when she wants to, even if that means spending more than the required $500. Remember, a happy au pair means happy children, and happy children mean a happy you.

KiKi from Japan used the educational requirement to further her career goals. When she came to the States, she had a serious interest in fashion and chose to be in the New York City area so she could really learn about the American fashion industry. She had a career ambition to start a clothing line in Japan when she returned home. To realize this goal, KiKi needed to learn how to organize and conduct fashion shows.

She found a course at FIT in New York City. It was a non-credit course called "Special Events for Fashion" and taught students how a runway fashion show worked. KiKi loved it and connected with the professor, who took a special interest in her. Before long, KiKi was going to the city regularly to serve as a "dresser" at real fashion shows. She would wear a waist pack with two-sided tape, safety pins, hairspray, and other tricks of the trade. Today, KiKi has a successful fashion line and comes to New York City twice a year to show her collection. Sure enough, she uses FIT students as the "dressers."

Holidays and the Au Pair

Whether you are Christian, Jewish, Buddhist, or Muslim, your holiday celebrations define you as a family. Including your au pair in your holiday celebrations is important to a successful cultural exchange. At the same time, you should invite your au pair to bring her cultural traditions into your holiday celebration. It will never be the same!

Because your au pair will be feeling extra sentimental (i.e., homesick) around the holidays, let her know as soon as possible what the family plans will be. Will you be traveling? Having family or friends to your house? Jetting off on a family vacation? Regardless of your plans, be clear with your au pair about when she will be included and when you will have just family time.

Every Thanksgiving morning, there is an 8K turkey trot run just up the street from my house. It has become a big family tradition. We run and then eat guilt-free for the rest of the day. I let my au pair know about the run well in advance, so that if she would like, she can begin to train for the run and truly be a part of this family tradition.

When the December holidays come around, there are a few things to keep in mind. If the true origins of Santa are a secret in your house, tell the au pair. The Santa myth varies tremendously from country to country, so be sure to talk to your au pair if you want your kids to still believe after Christmas morning.

Be sure that there are presents for your au pair. I prefer to stock envelopes with gift cards, but I have also made photo scrapbooks, which are always a big hit. If your kids are crafty, homemade presents are always welcome. If you celebrate with stockings, be sure to have one filled for your au pair.

Encourage Her Dreams

Figure out what dreams fill your au pair's head. Does she want to run a hotel one day? Or go to medical school? Does she want to play professional soccer? Or be a model? Does she really, really want to find an American boyfriend?

To have a good year with your au pair, it is in your best interest to learn what these dreams are and then encourage them. Very few au pairs want to watch children for forty-five hours per week for the rest of their lives. They have joined the au pair program for other reasons. You will have the best experience with your au pair if you can figure these out and do your best to make them happen.

At nineteen or twenty years old, few au pairs know what they want to be when they grow up. They have chosen to be an au pair to help them figure it out or to avoid the question entirely. Once in a host family's home, most au pairs are reluctant to admit that child care is not their passion. On their application forms, they professed to "love children!" and they want you to believe that they are 100% committed to their job.

Be patient with your au pair and give her the space and the opportunity to discuss her aspirations openly. Once she opens up, your job will be easier. You can then help her find classes that might further her goals. You can also be on the lookout for other opportunities in your community that will widen her horizons.

The bottom line is that an au pair can do both. She can provide great child care for you *and* realize her dreams (whatever they may be). There is room for both in the au pair–host family relationship. If you are encouraging and open, while at the same time communicative about her household responsibilities, the program is a win-win.

Understanding your au pair's dreams and then facilitating them can be great training for parenting your own children (when they finally become young adults), so pay attention! If you build a trustful, communicative relationship with your au pair, she will believe that you want the best for her. She will feel respected. She will value your family and love your children even more. She will be a better au pair.

But Know if She Has a Secret Agenda

You should encourage your au pair to explore her dreams. But at the same time, it is important to know if she has plans to stay in the States – legally or not. Get to know your au pair and listen to her when she talks about her long-term goals. Will she return to her home country? Will she stay in the United States? Does she want to go to university? Does she want to marry an American and live in a big house?

If you have a great au pair, you can encourage her to extend her program year by six, nine, or twelve months. Some families will sponsor their au pair's full-time student Visa and help her go to college while still providing child care.

If she does want to stay in the United States (as your childcare provider or not), the most important thing you can do is help her make plans that will allow her to stay legally. Au pairs who stay in the U.S. illegally get into loads of trouble.

TIP: Figure out if your au pair has plans to stay in the country after the program. If she is going to stay, encourage her to stay legally.

I was too naïve with Vera to see that she was planning for the whole year to stay in the United States. If I could have that au pair experience again, I would have definitely figured out earlier that she had no intention of going back home after her year.

Vera embodied the classic Eastern European stereotype of a person lacking emotion. She rarely smiled. She hardly laughed. Day to day, she was not particularly cheerful. She would do exactly what I asked, very competently. She was clean and efficient. She was a good driver. But she did not reveal very much about herself, and I don't think she liked my kids very much. I never once saw her snuggling on the couch with them, reading a story. I never once saw her give them a hug good night.

Early into her year, we discovered that despite her poor English, Vera was one very smart young woman. She had come to the U.S. with a plan. She did not particularly love children (though she was a competent au pair), but she did love learning. She took her job seriously and quickly mastered the daily routine. She would march Hank to school in a baby jogger, go for a run, and then get to work learning English.

Life can be challenging if you don't speak, don't smile, and aren't all that friendly. Before that fateful cluster event at the rock gym, Vera did not make a single friend. I would try to get her to talk to me, but she would answer in short, three-word sentences.

"You don't seem very happy," I prodded, trying to check in with her.

"I am fine," she answered.

"Is everything all right at home? Are you feeling homesick?" I tried to get further.

"Everything is fine. I am fine," she insisted, not showing any emotion whatsoever.

"Well, is there anything I can do to make you happier here?" I asked. "I really want you to be happy."

"No," she replied. "I am happy."

But she did not look very happy.

I admit that I was stumped. In the beginning, I had had such high hopes that Vera and I would be friends (I was, after all, the only other girl in the house). We were not all that dissimilar: we both liked sports; we were competitive, smart, and hardworking. Not to mention that we were both pretty darn short. I was disappointed that she was so private with her life. She never opened up to me, even though I tried. In fact, most of the time, I thought she was being secretive. I finally gave up trying. It was just too much effort. Vera kept marching.

The day came when it was time for her to leave, and she asked me to drive her to a house two towns over. Much to my surprise, she had landed a job working as a live-in sitter for a family. She had done her homework. With a new student visa, she enrolled in the local university and spent the next five years working toward her degree.

Get 'Er out There: Au Pair Travel

From the same secret handbook where they learn to say "I love children," all au pairs arrive in the United States with a list of mandatory trips. They all want to see New York City (of course), but the other destinations are not so obvious. The list includes Niagara Falls, Atlantic City, Boston, and Philadelphia. Las Vegas with a day trip to the Grand Canyon is on the list, as is anywhere in California. Many want to see Florida, and Miami in particular. On their salary, au pairs look for the most inexpensive travel possible. You will need to help get your au pair started by sharing information on cheap travel options.

TIP: Check out Cultural Highways and Trek America; they are national youth travel organizations frequented by au pairs. The companies run inexpensive tours all over the United States.

Kit was an adventurous au pair. During her year with us, she went to Niagara Falls, Philadelphia, Boston, San Francisco, Los Angeles, Hollywood, the Grand Canyon, and Las Vegas. Her favorite was Las Vegas. She would save her money for a month or so, and when she had just enough, off she would go. She would come home broke and exhausted, ready to save up again for the next trip.

> *TIP: Au pairs often stay at youth hostels. Check out hiusa.org for information on hostelling.*

Sally would troll Web sites for two-day tours from NYC. Buses left from Chinatown and went to Boston, Niagara Falls, Baltimore, and Montreal. Niagara Falls is a must-see for all au pairs; for $99 per person, an au pair can do a two-day bus tour to Niagara Falls, a Maid of the Mist boat tour at the falls, museum entrance to the Corning, NY, Glass Museum, and a night at a motel. If there are four au pairs going together, they can all share a room. What a bargain. But they have to like sitting on a bus. These are long bus rides.

During her year with us, Sally took trips to Niagara Falls, Boston, Philadelphia, and Atlantic City on Chinatown buses with her friends. She went to Miami, Florida, with her boyfriend, Andy.

Sally and Andy got inexpensive plane tickets and made reservations at the youth hostel on South Beach. Who knew that there was a youth hostel on South Beach? Knowing that it was likely to be a college spring break week, I had cautioned Sally that it would be crowded and that they should make reservations early. My other piece of advice was that they should bring lots of sunscreen. I even bought her a big bottle. She was blonde and fair, and I figured she would burn easily.

They took the sunscreen to Miami, but it must have gotten buried in their suitcase. Sally reported that the first day was overcast and cloudy, and they spent the day walking the streets of Miami sightseeing. They next day, they went to the beach to sunbathe. They completely fried themselves and spent the next several days taking cold showers at the youth hostel to stop the sunburn pain. When they arrived back to New Jersey, they had peeling faces, smiles, and seemed as mellow as ever. The trip—from their perspective—had been a resounding success, and I still had a full bottle of sunscreen.

Au pairs are allowed to travel outside the United States during their year; however, there is a lot of paperwork required, and they have to work closely with their sponsoring agency. So if your au pair wants to go to the Canadian side of Niagara Falls, she needs to plan the trip well in advance!

Au pairs are also allowed to stay in the United States for an additional month on their J-1 visa. Many au pairs use this 13th month to travel.

Farewells

Memories of a great year in America are the best thing that your au pair will take home with her. If your au pair has wended her way into your hearts and you will miss her, however, you may want to show her your appreciation for a job well done.

A few ideas for going-away gifts include a photo scrapbook or collage, jewelry with your kids' names engraved, or a locket with their picture. Because au pairs don't make a lot of money and love to shop, you may want to consider a cash gift at the end. We try to make our au pair's last night special by taking her out to dinner (without the kids) or by hosting a big family dinner or a party with some of her friends.

One host family gives their au pair two tickets to a Broadway show one night before she leaves. Another will send her home with all her favorite American foods.

The most important farewell you can make is to say thank you to your au pair and share with her how much you value her contribution to your family. Whether that contribution was teaching your children another language, sharing a favorite game or song, or just going twelve months without a car accident, say thank you. It means a lot.

CHAPTER 5:

THE ART OF THE REMATCH – WHEN THINGS GO WRONG

Not every match between an au pair and host family is a success. The au pair agencies will tell you that only about one in ten matches ends in a rematch. I have found that the statistic is true, except I have always been in the minority. My sister-in-law had au pairs for ten years with only one rematch. I know some families who have never rematched. We have not been that lucky.

When you make the unfortunate decision to rematch, you will work closely with your local coordinator to find a new au pair. First, she will assure you that a bad match does not mean that your family is bad or that the au pair is bad, just that you are not compatible. A rematch is not a failure, and you should not think it is. Families and au pairs, after all, commit to a relationship without ever having met in person. It's a crapshoot. Most matches do work. Some don't.

There are four main reasons for rematching: mismatch, miscommunication, misbehavior, and life.

Mismatch

In this situation, both the au pair and the host family agree to part ways. When this happens, the au pair remains living with the family until the family finds a new au pair or until the au pair finds a new family. It is an amicable divorce.

Andrea from Brazil was smart, accomplished, and organized. But she was wrong, wrong, wrong for our family. She was a girly-girl who wore lots of makeup and had a hard time relating to my young, active boys. She liked to do arts and crafts, and my boys liked to play hide-and-seek. She liked to have formal sit-down meals with china and linens. My boys preferred picnics.

Two other things contributed to the mismatch. Andrea had the very bad luck of arriving during one of the coldest spells in history. This sweet girl from tropical Brazil arrived in NYC in subzero temperatures. She might as well have flown to Mars. Also, her English was not great. She communicated with me just fine, but she had a very difficult time understanding my boys. The boys could not understand a word that she said. She was miserable in my house. I was sad for her.

All through the first month, we talked with Andrea a lot about how difficult the adjustment was for her and for the boys. After the trip to Sante Fe, we knew it was not going to work. There was just no chemistry. Andrea had been with us for about five weeks when we rematched. She went to a family in southern New Jersey with three girls. She had a terrific year with this family, playing tea parties and dress-up and doing hair and makeup. Andrea extended for a second year and was a great au pair for her new family.

TIP: Consider climate when choosing an au pair. If you live in the snowbelt, an au pair from the tropics will require a significant adjustment. Discuss in the interview how your climate might be a challenge for your au pair.

Miscommunication

In this scenario, the au pair requests a rematch. This might happen because the family is making her work more than the forty-five hours per week or because she does not have as much freedom as she expected. When this happens, usually the au pair stays with the host family while trying to find a new situation.

To avoid this type of rematch, you must be brutally honest with your au pair in the interview process. In addition to the deal-breaker questions, you have to be clear on key issues such as work hours, use of the car, house rules, the temperament of your children, the climate in which you live, and the household dynamic. If you have a daughter with a temper, don't sugarcoat it. Tell it like it is. If you will not allow your au pair to have friends over to your home, tell her that before she arrives. Honesty during the interview process is the first step toward a successful match.

We have never had an au pair request a rematch. But we have gotten an au pair who had requested a rematch before. Our Japanese au pair, KiKi, came to us from a family in rural California. The family was a Japanese-American family with two small children. They did not allow KiKi the use of their car, and the family asked her to speak only Japanese to the children. These were two issues that they had not fully discussed during the interview process. KiKi had felt duped. She had grimly looked forward to her year living with that host family—difficulty meeting other au pairs because she was not able to get out of the house and not learning English because she was required to speak her native language at home. This was not her idea of a cultural exchange. She requested a rematch, went to live with a friend in San Francisco, and then found us. KiKi was a fabulous au pair, and we had a great cultural exchange.

Misbehavior

If the au pair misbehaves, shows poor judgment, or just plain stinks at her job, the host family can request the rematch. In this instance, the au pair is simply fired and usually goes to live with the coordinator until she finds a new family.

Lena made a horrible first impression. During her very first weekend with us, she got sloppy drunk at a family party and announced that she was going to jump off a balcony. We stopped her (of course) and gave her a warning. STRIKE 1. Several weeks later, Lena came down to work with the shakes (having partied the night before). STRIKE 2. Later that day, she let my boys watch the PG-13-rated movie *xXx*. And WHY had she let them watch that movie? I asked. Because it was filmed in Prague (her home city) and because she thought Vin Diesel was sexy. STRIKE 3. She was out. We went into rematch.

We did have an au pair who just plain stunk at her job. That was Jin Hee, also known as Carla (au pairs from South Korea pick English names for themselves). Carla was a terrible driver; she would have only Korean friends; and she was very picky about her diet, insisting on authentic Korean food. Once, she completely missed picking up the kids at school because she had driven one hour away to meet a friend and lost track of time. She was apathetic about our young dog and often forgot to put the dog in her crate when she left the house. I lost an antique chair and countless shoes to the dog's unsupervised mornings. The final straw with Carla was her indifference to my boys. Will fell down the stairs one day (during an unusually intense game of hide-and-seek) and broke his arm. He called me in hysterics, then administered his own first aid, and only then did he tell Carla, who was IMing her friends on the family computer.

Life Happens

Sometimes events happen that will force your au pair to leave before the end of the year-long commitment. Opportunity will knock. Strange events will occur.

Bobby was a very tall, handsome kid from Hamburg; he had a Justin-Timberlake-plus-ten-inches look. He joined the au pair program because he had not gotten into the graphic design program of his choice. Once in New York City, though, he was often stopped on the street. "Are you a model?" people would ask. "Did I see you on TV?" A seed was planted.

I encouraged the hobby, not thinking it would actually amount to anything. There are thousands of aspiring models in NYC. What were the chances of Bobby making it? But it kept him busy during the day, and he never let his hobby interfere with his duties of taking care of his two kids in the suburbs.

Bobby Googled "modeling agency" + "new york city" and got a list. The next day, he dropped off the kids at school at 8:30 a.m. and hopped on the 8:46 a.m. train to NYC. At 9:30 that morning, he walked into a modeling agency and was signed on the spot. Things started happening quickly after that. Bobby had an agent who called him several times a day.

Several days a week, he went into the city and attended "go sees" and casting calls. At first, he did a few runway shows for very urban clothing lines.

Because of his J-1 visa, Bobby could not be paid in dollars for his work, so he came up with an alternative way to be compensated for his modeling: He was paid in clothing.

"This stuff is really not me," he told me when he came home with his first in-kind paycheck: a bright white denim jacket, matching baggy pants complete with an oversized cap. So Bobby did what anyone would have done: He auctioned the clothes on eBay. After several successful transactions, Bobby bought himself a kick-ass digital camera.

Several months after he had arrived, Bobby booked a photo shoot for a print ad with the rapper S. Carter for Reebok. It appeared on the back cover of *Vibe* magazine. One month later, he was invited to move to Milan for "the Collections." With both reluctance and pride, we encouraged him to go, knowing that it was truly a once-in-a-lifetime opportunity. He had been with the family for six months.

The Process of Rematching

From the first day, when you pick up your au pair, the local coordinator is documenting how things are going. You will get a call within forty-eight hours and a visit in your home within a week. The local coordinator will talk with you and with the au pair about first impressions, about the adjustment, and about the children. If things are not hunky-dory after a week, the local coordinator is going to encourage you to keep at it. Unless something unusual has happened (i.e., a car accident), the agency does not want you to go into rematch until everyone has given the match a good try. This is usually about three to four weeks. Throughout that time, the local coordinator will be documenting her weekly contacts with you and the au pair and may even try a mediation session to resolve differences. If, after four weeks, you and/or the au pair are still miserable, you can officially go into rematch.

At this point, if you have made the decision to rematch, you will need to inform your au pair that you are rematching. Assuming that it is a regular mismatch ("we're just not right for each other"), you should assure your au pair that the rematch is not her fault. Sometimes there is just a mismatch. Tell her that you know she will be happier with a different family. Be confident in the decision. She *will* be happier with a new family. Speak slowly and in short sentences.

Per usual, your kids are a step ahead of you, and they have already sensed that things are not great with the new au pair. So next, you need to tell your children about the rematch. In that conversation, do not disparage the au pair to your kids. Tell them that she is going to find a new family where she will be happier and that you are getting a new au pair who will fit in better with your family. Assure them that it is not their fault and you are not angry with them. Tell them that it was not your au pair's fault and that you are not angry with her. It just didn't work out. With a new au pair, you are sure that your kids will be happier and that your family will be happier. Speak slowly and in short sentences.

The Floater Pool
To get a new au pair, you look in the "floater pool." The floater pool is an ever-changing collective list of au pairs "in-country" or located across the nation in search of new host

families. In most cases, the agency wants the au pairs to stay local, even within the same cluster. The agency wants to keep them close to the friends they have established. Also, they really do not want to pay for the airfare of getting an au pair from the West Coast to the East Coast. At any time, there are about twenty to thirty au pairs in the floater pool.

There are two types of au pairs in the floater pool: those who are rematching and those who are extending for their second year. The pressure is on for those who are rematching: they have exactly two weeks to find a new family, or they must return to their home country.

The extension au pairs are finishing their first year and want to rematch with a new family for a second year. In most cases, this is because they want to see and experience a different part of the country. This could be a great option for you, because the au pair has been through the adjustment, she has decided that she does like children (at least well enough), her English will be great, and she understands the job. Au pairs who are extending will hit the floater pool a month or so in advance. If you are in a hurry to find an au pair, it is unlikely that an extension au pair will join your family quickly. In my last rematch, I spoke with a girl in Virginia who had completed her first year and wanted to extend for a second year. Having spent a year in Virginia, she had decided that for her second year, she wanted to go to California to experience another region of the United States. Needless to say, I could not even begin to convince her to move to New Jersey. Can you blame her?

The Online Search
You look for rematch au pairs the same way you look for a new au pair—using the online search tool. You see the au

pair's original application including her pictures, profile, and essay. Most important, you read notes from the agency on why the au pair is in the rematch pool. The notes are written by the local coordinator responsible for the rematch au pair. The comments are professional and tactful, so you need to read between the lines.

For example, if you read "The au pair and the host family disagreed on scheduling and household responsibilities," the au pair is probably a diva. She wants to be in charge. She needs attention. Look for someone else. You do not want a high-maintenance au pair.

If you read "The au pair had trouble communicating with the small children," this probably means that the au pair cannot speak or understand English well. If you read "The au pair had a small fender bender in the grocery store parking lot," this probably means that the au pair is a terrible driver.

Sometimes, the au pair is in the rematch pool even though she is a great au pair. You may come across a note stating, "The family is experiencing financial difficulty and can no longer keep the au pair."

If you are rematching, the agency will not allow you to speak to the former host family. This is not negotiable. Because rematches occur for many reasons—mostly highly emotional—the agency communicates reasons for the rematch professionally and impartially. Sure, there are crazy au pairs, but there are some crazy families, too. The agency will provide facts but no sordid details. Remember, they want to keep as many au pairs and host families in the program as possible. They have invested time and money to get the au pair into the program, so when the au pair goes home, the agency loses money. The vast majority of au pairs in the rematch pool will find a more compatible situation. And that host family might be yours.

Financial Implications

Financially, rematching is complicated, and each agency has different policies. When you rematch, you are required to pay for the additional months that your new au pair has on her year. Read the fine print or speak to your local coordinator about the financial implications of rematching.

Keep Your Chin up

Look on the bright side: Rematching has its benefits. The au pair has already adjusted to living away from home. You will not have to endure the five weeks of au pair adjustment. She may have been with a crazy family and will appreciate how sane you are and how charming your children are. Your new au pair will be grateful that she is not being sent home and is now living with a normal family. She will try very, very hard to make her new au pair experience a success.

CHAPTER 6:
WHY IT'S WORTH IT

I know you are wondering why I have stayed with it. Why do I keep getting au pairs? Am I crazy? Wouldn't my life be easier if I just got off the au pair treadmill? Try a live-in, I hear you telling me, some nice woman from the islands. She won't be here legally, of course, but she might keep your house just a little cleaner than it is right now. Get someone a bit more mature, who needs the money and won't skip out on you when she gets homesick. Someone who won't ding the car or go out every night partying.

Believe me, I've thought about it. There are just really good reasons to stay with the au pair program. Health insurance, for one.

Health Insurance

When Karen from South Africa was our au pair, I learned why it is so important to be in the au pair program. The week before Christmas that year, Karen came downstairs and asked me if I could recommend a dentist. She was having pain in her mouth. She said that it was not quite a toothache—more like a pain in the jaw underneath her teeth. Karen assured me that she had had her teeth completely checked before she had come to the States. She still had her wisdom teeth. Maybe they were the problem. I was working from home that day, scheduled to go to the holiday concert at Hank's school, so I took advantage of being home and called our dentist. She told us to come by right away. Au pairs do have health insurance through the program, though I had no idea if it covered dental work.

Dr. Laura took an x-ray of Karen's mouth but could not see anything wrong. Just to be safe, she suggested that we see an oral surgeon. She even called and arranged an appointment for later that day. An avid bird-watcher and eco-traveler, Dr. Laura loved talking with Karen about African animals and travel. She didn't charge me a dime.

We drove from the dentist's office to the oral surgeon's office. He did an x-ray of her mouth and concluded that perhaps she was clenching and grinding her teeth at night and that temporomandibular joint disorder (TMJ) or simple muscle cramps were the cause of the pain. He prescribed a muscle relaxant and a painkiller and sent us off to the holiday concert, where Hank wore reindeer antlers and sang like an angel.

TIP: Dental insurance is not included in the program. Tell your au pair to have a complete dental checkup and cleaning before she comes to the United States.

The next day, Karen was no better. In fact, the pain was getting worse, and her jaw was beginning to swell. But she was as cheerful as she could be, even decorating Christmas candy houses with us late into the night. The next day, she was even more swollen. Her boyfriend, Brian, came by first thing in the morning to take her back to the oral surgeon. This time, the oral surgeon said that she needed a root canal. He sent her off to a very grumpy endodontist who performed the root canal and rushed out of the office to go to California for the holidays. It was December 22.

Over the next several days, Brian earned his place in the boyfriend hall of fame. Not only did he take Karen to the endodontist and wait with her through the procedure, but he talked with the various doctors, brought her home, and sat with her until she fell asleep. He was extremely attentive.

The next day was December 23, and we were preparing for a big family celebration. Despite the ice packs, the antibiotics, and the painkiller, Karen's face was still scarily swollen. It was an odd countenance: a fashion model beauty with a goiter the size of an apple on her neck. The oral surgeon and the endodontist told her it was a normal reaction to a root canal; the swelling would subside.

Karen attended our holiday family dinner with her goiter and a smile. She couldn't eat but managed to sip a glass of eggnog and still played games with the kids. She even chatted with my sister-in-law's new au pair from Turkey. Brian stopped by late that evening to pick up Karen. They had tickets to the Christmas Eve football game at the Meadowlands the next day. We talked about how we all thought she should be feeling and looking better. Shouldn't the swelling be going down? We all agreed that another good night's sleep would do it.

Karen went to Brian's house that night, the day before the football game. Before she left, we told her all about American football and the joys of tailgate parties. She was looking forward to this truly American experience. But at 8 a.m. the next day, Brian called me. Karen couldn't speak. The swelling had extended to her tongue. She was having trouble breathing. Her chest hurt. "Get her to the hospital! Call the oral surgeon!" They left the house and went straight to the hospital.

Karen was admitted to the hospital and put on steroids, a super antibiotic, and painkillers. There was now a very serious infection in her jawbone. They did not know the cause of the infection but knew that it was bad and it was spreading to her lungs. An infectious disease specialist was called in. Karen was from Africa, so they were taking no chances, thinking that it might be some strange, exotic ailment.

Brian stayed at her side nearly the whole time: all through Christmas Eve and through Christmas Day, only leaving when the security guard kicked him out at night.

Karen spent her first Christmas in the United States in a hospital bed in Bloomfield, New Jersey. The day after Christmas, she spiked a fever of 104 degrees, and they decided that they had to do surgery. The question was, could they get to the infection through her mouth, or would they have to go in through the outside of her face? She was in a panic, thinking that her dreams of acting and modeling were about to be ruined by a huge scar along her jawline.

We talked with the surgeon, who said that he thought he could do it through her mouth, but there was no time for discussion. They had to go in and get this thing … now. In a two-hour surgery, they removed a tooth (which had been killed by the infection) to get down to the part of the jaw with the infection. They removed a huge cyst from the jaw and drained her face of the fluid that had built up. She was out of it for another day, but slowly, the swelling went down. She was finally getting better.

I sent Mark and the boys to Vermont, where we were scheduled to meet friends after the holidays. I stayed home and spent time with Karen in the hospital. Three days later, I brought her home, still with some swelling but definitely getting better every day.

Brian, his friends, and his family sent a steady stream of cards, flowers, stuffed animals, and visitors. She talked with her mom and her grandmother every day. Her dad and her brothers called on Christmas Day. Thousands of miles from home, Karen was well loved, and she knew it.

In ten days, Karen had had several x-rays, one emergency root canal, one emergency room visit, fifty blood tests, a dozen IV bags, maxillofacial surgery, serious pain medication, and one very devoted boyfriend. As I thought about the situation, I could only imagine what the hospital bill would be—tens of thousands of dollars, for sure. We never saw the bill. The au pair health insurance, which we had never once needed in the past, completely covered the bill, minus the $100 co-pay (that I happily paid).

I asked myself a very selfish question: What would we have done if she did not have health insurance? What would we have done if she had been just a regular nanny, in the country illegally and without health insurance? Well, I answered, we would have paid the bill, of course, probably in monthly installments for the rest of our lives. So I was never more grateful for paying that annual fee to the au pair agency, which covers the health insurance for the au pair. In almost five years and with nine au pairs, we had never even had a doctor's visit. But man, did we need it with Karen. I would never consider going outside the program again.

A Global Perspective

I have stayed with the au pair program for more than just the health insurance. By having au pairs, I believe that my kids will have a more global outlook on the world, be more interesting people and more open to those who are different. I believe that I am a better parent because I have had au pairs.

I think it is good for my kids to get to know and come to love people from different backgrounds, cultures, and customs. Kit from New Zealand is a great example. Even though I had very little in common with Kit, she was a great fit for the boys. They played together, watched TV together, and during the summer, swam at the town pool together. She loved my boys. There is no doubt about that. And they loved her.

To me, Kit was always sloppy and sometimes immature, but she was loveable. Kit would cook her dinner and leave her dishes and pots soaking in the sink. She always looked rumpled and disheveled, even though I noticed a steady stream of new T-shirts and pants. She never combed her hair, leaving the blonde curls to just stick out this way or that. Her acne never cleared up after that critical week four. She ate slices and slices of potato bread and her share of Oreos. It took a major effort to get the boys and Kit to clean the playroom. And when they did, the result was a cleared space of carpet surrounded by towers of toys. Nothing was put away in the cabinets or on the shelves. It was impossible to find anything again. She never mastered how to read the monthly calendar and needed constant reminders about who needed to go where when. She could never remember the names of the kids' friends—instead referring to them by their looks. Will's best friend Billy was "the tall boy with glasses." Hank's friend Johnny was "the Chinese boy," even though he was biracial and not really Chinese. And she could never remember where anyone lived. I would remind her, and she would look at me, smile, laugh, and say, "Oh, that's right! Now I remember!" Will became an excellent navigator in the car.

I found these foibles annoying but reminded myself that the boys loved her. She was reliable and caring. That was the most important thing.

One summer night at the beach, we were sitting on the porch, looking at the sunset when Will noticed the big yellow full moon rising over the beach in the east as the sun set in the west. He pointed it out to all of us.

"Look! Mom! Dad! Look at the moon!" he shouted, delighted that he was the first to notice it.

"Just think, Kit," my mother-in-law said to her, "that same moon is just setting in New Zealand."

"The same moon?" She paused. "Is it really?" She looked very puzzled.

We didn't quite know what to say. We were sure there was only one moon, and it was indeed the same moon visible in the Southern Hemisphere. Could she have really thought that there was a different moon in New Zealand? I was speechless. My mother-in-law came to the rescue.

"Yes, dear. It is the very same one. We live in a very small world. Very small, indeed."

Will gave Kit a pat on the head.

KiKi, our au pair from Japan, came from a culture that was very different from ours. Because she was a part of their lives, my boys now respect and have a curiosity for Japanese things. Things they learn in school about Japan come alive because they know someone from that country. They have learned that just because people do things differently, they are not wrong or bad. Living with KiKi enriched our lives in a way that simply would not have been possible without her.

For example, KiKi did all of her cooking with chopsticks. Chopsticks were the only kitchen utensil that I ever saw her use. She made scrambled eggs with chopsticks, stirred soup with chopsticks, and showed us that the very best way to get toast out of the toaster was to use chopsticks. Will and Hank became expert chopstick users, even learning how to eat french fries with chopsticks. We still use chopsticks in the toaster today.

KiKi changed our family traditions. For Thanksgiving that year, KiKi created the most unbelievable sushi and sashimi platter for our family feast in Philadelphia. While Mark, the boys, and I ran the annual turkey trot race, KiKi spent all morning carefully constructing rolls, pieces of sushi, and carefully crafted pieces of art made from vegetables. She wrapped the platter gently in plastic wrap and held it on her lap for the entire two-hour drive. Once there, KiKi gracefully presented the platter to the assembled family with a bow and then beamed the rest of the day. We all ate so much sushi that afterward, we were not all that hungry for turkey. And in the years since KiKi left, we have always served sushi as a first course at Thanksgiving dinner in her honor.

Whenever Hank was out of line, KiKi would bend down to him, tickle him behind his ears, look right in his eyes, and smile at him, telling him firmly what she wanted him to do. Unlike any previous au pair, KiKi had a way with Hank. He responded to and obeyed her.

KiKi taught the boys some Japanese. She called Hank "Anku." "Sai sha gu, jhong king pong" is "rock, paper, scissors, shoot" in Japanese … or something like that. I would regularly find KiKi and the boys playing this game together. Even several years after KiKi left, I've often found the boys resolving a dispute with rock-paper-scissors—in Japanese.

Our experience with KiKi made me realize what having a great au pair was supposed to be like. This was a true cultural exchange. My kids loved her and were now fascinated with and interested in Japanese culture, cuisine, and history. In turn, KiKi perfected her English and made explorations into her future career. She was appreciative of everything we did for her, and I was appreciative of her. She was organized and reliable. She loved my kids.

Au Pairs Can Help with Family Transitions

Dramatic family events happen: the loss of a job, the death of a family member or pet, etc. How your au pair responds to these stressful situations often determines whether she will be remembered as a great au pair. Sally cemented herself into our family during a transition in our pets, from our dog Maggie to our puppy Ginger.

Our old dog Maggie was over-the-moon-in-love with Sally. After I got home every day, Sally would put a leash on our eleven-year-old yellow Lab and take her for a long, slow walk. Sally's ulterior motive for her walk was to smoke cigarettes, but I did not care.

A yellow lab who had flunked out of seeing-eye dog school, Maggie was a wonderful family dog, but she was failing. She would stumble walking up or down the stairs. She was losing weight, and her ribs poked through her yellowish-white fur. Cataracts had fuzzied her eyes. She slept a lot.

Sally was kind and sweet to the old dog. Each day around six, Maggie would rally from her daylong nap for her evening constitutional with Sally. Sally was our very first au pair to actually take a serious interest in our dog. Walking the dog was not part of Sally's job description, but she took on this responsibility, and it soon became part of the family routine.

As Mark and I watched Maggie's declining health, we often discussed the dilemma that we would face when Maggie finally died (which we knew would be in the not-so-distant future). We are a dog family. We have always had a dog. There was just no question in our minds that we would get another dog. We could not imagine our house without a dog. But with both of us working in New York City full-time, we struggled with how we would manage to raise a puppy.

Sally came at the perfect time. She loved dogs, and as we shared our sadness at seeing Maggie dying, Sally was the first one to suggest that we get a puppy. She offered to take care of it. She was home during the day, and she could take it for walks and train it. This was a perfect solution. A puppy might even give Maggie some added energy in the last days of her life.

The boys soon had a new hobby: combing the *Encyclopedia of Dogs* with Sally. Together, they would put yellow sticky notes on any profile that seemed to match—or not. For about two weeks, Hank insisted that the perfect dog for us was an Alaskan malamute. I reminded him how hot it could get in New Jersey in the summer and of the fact that such a dog needed to be outside for a lot of exercise. Our third-of-an-acre suburban lot would just not give an Alaskan malamute enough room to run. Will wanted a German shepherd. I had grown up with shepherds, and I knew that they shed a lot. No way! I quickly dismissed any dog that shed a lot of hair. We took online compatibility tests to find the perfect dog for us. Soon, the encyclopedia was covered in yellow sticky notes. In the end, we came back to where we had started—we wanted a retreiver: yellow, brown, or black. We surfed breeders' Web sites and exchanged e-mails to find litters that were for sale.

On a very cold day in February, a few weeks before Mark's fortieth birthday, we all piled into the car and drove to southern New Jersey. At Red Lions Kennels in the middle of New Jersey farmland, we met Kate, the breeder, and her five Chesapeake Bay retriever puppies: three males and two females. We wanted a girl dog. So from the two females, we picked out Ginger, a squiggly ball of curly brown fur, with gigantic light-brown eyes and big paws. Full grown, a Chessie, as they are known, look like a curly-haired chocolate lab. They grow to be about seventy-five pounds, have big light-brown eyes, floppy ears, and wavy coats. They are great swimmers. According to Kate, the breeder, Chesapeake Bay retrievers are good family dogs but are known for being a bit stubborn and protective. You have to show them who is boss. Sally listened attentively. She sat in the backseat with the boys for the drive home. Little Ginger sat on her lap and threw up on her the whole way home. Sally gave her pets and kisses the entire ride, whispering to her that everything would be all right.

Sally welcomed Ginger with as much enthusiasm as the boys did. She spoiled Ginger to death. During the day, Sally would take Ginger for two or three walks. She would sit at the computer and answer e-mails or talk to her boyfriend on Skype with Ginger in her lap. Sally taught Ginger to sit, to lie down, and to give her a paw. Despite being gaga over the new puppy, Sally did not abandon her devotion to Maggie. At 6:00 every night, Sally took Maggie out for their slow, long walk. She was hospice care for our old dog, and I am forever grateful to her.

Sally's big moment came on the day we decided to put Maggie down. The day before, Maggie had had a massive seizure on our dining room floor. Ginger had nuzzled her neck while Maggie was sleeping, trying to get her to rally and play. As she was lying on her side, Maggie's limbs went into rigid convulsions. She foamed at the mouth and peed all over the floor. It was horrible to watch. But it was a clear sign that it was time to make the decision that we had been avoiding all spring.

We went round and round and could not figure out who should go and who should stay home. I was not thinking clearly. Mark was not thinking clearly. Will kept insisting on coming along. I wasn't sure he could handle it. I wasn't sure I could handle it. I knew for sure that Hank should not go. Sally, Mark, and I discussed the different scenarios. It was rational, levelheaded, compassionate Sally who came up with the solution. She took Hank to the park with Ginger. They played until the sun went down. Mark, Will, and I took Maggie to the vet. Afterward, we all met up for dinner and cried, especially Sally.

Training for the Teen Years

Being a host parent can also provide ideal training ground for parenting a teenager. As a host parent, you are responsible for some level of "parenting" such as weighing in on the benefits of dating, helping to organize educational opportunities, or teaching a new driver the rules of the car.

Bobby gave me a glimpse of how completely unprepared I was to parent a teenage boy. Bobby came to me one day and asked me if it would be OK with me if he asked a local girl to go to the movies with him. I got a lump in my throat. My heart was racing. I panicked. My thoughts wandered. Why had Bobby asked me for permission? I didn't see a problem with Bobby going on a date with a girl. Did I? I was flustered and confused.

I asked him some ridiculously embarrassing questions: Would he pay? Would she pay? Would they "go dutch"? Who would drive? Where would they go? Would he pick her up or meet her there? How old was she? Where did she live? Did I know her parents? Did her parents know me? What if they started dating? Would her parents blame me if she fell in love with the handsome German male au pair? What if she moved to Germany? What if he broke her heart? Would she blame me? Would her parents blame me? Was I to blame?

I had no idea what the right answer was to any of the questions. What I didn't want was for the whole town to think that my au pair was hanging around town, picking up girls.

I reminded myself that Bobby was twenty-one years old and that I had promised to treat him like an adult. Mark assured me that this was not something to stress out about. It was no big deal. I took a deep breath.

"Go on the date," I told him. "Have fun." For the first and only time in my years of having an au pair, I stayed up until

Bobby got home from the movies. They went on exactly one date. I don't know what happened because I was too embarrassed to ask.

Hopefully, when Will and Hank are old enough to ask my opinion about whether they should ask a girl to the movies, I will react just a little more rationally.

With my background of experiences teaching driving skills to my au pairs, I am much more confident for my kids to start driving than dating. It is quite possible that they will be far better drivers than many of my au pairs. First, there was Kit, who smooshed the side of the car against the house. Then KiKi drove over the cement bumper in the parking lot at the mall. And Helen took the front bumper off the car while navigating the local parking garage.

I now know just how I will react when one of my boys has his first fender bender. I will be sanguine, encouraging him to try harder next time, to please use the side mirrors, and to know that the objects are closer than they appear. I will be grateful, knowing that nobody was hurt. I just hope that the Volvo lasts that long. I may not be so forgiving if we have a new car!

FINAL THOUGHTS

So I haven't scared you off, and you might actually think this program might work for your family? Welcome to the club. Here's some final advice.

Communicate. The key ingredient to a successful host family–au pair relationship is honest communication. From the initial phone call to the introductory e-mail to your first face-to-face meeting, communicating honestly with your au pair is the single most important thing you can do to make the relationship work. Although it is vitally important in the beginning of the year, you have to keep at it. Ongoing check-ins and proactive resolution of issues that arise are important for a rewarding cultural exchange.

Don't debate. When the time comes for you to look through the candidates, call overseas, and interview prospective au pairs, remember that you just have to choose one. The truth is that it is a crapshoot. Someone who looks great on paper may be lousy in real life. Someone who sounds great on the phone might be a terrible au pair. Some au pairs have completely unrealistic expectations. It's a risk. So pick one who has a friendly smile, nice handwriting, or pretty photos. If you like stickers, pick one who puts cute stickers on her application. Go with your gut. If all else fails, do rock-paper-scissors in a foreign language.

Start with a clean slate. I think back to the experience we had with Vera with some regret. She was our first au pair, and for a year, we delicately danced around many of the issues that should have been addressed head-on. We didn't communicate well. I should have pushed harder to include her in our family activities. When she said "no," I should have insisted. I should have weaseled my way into her personal life to get to know her better. "So who is that boy who keeps calling?" I never got a straight answer from her, and I should have kept asking the question. I think we would have been happier and she would have been happier. So if your first au pair is just so-so, try again. Start with a clean slate. Keep at it. It is not you, or your au pair, or the program. It just takes a while to get the hang of it.

Appreciate. Say "thank you" to your au pair. This is what your au pair wants to hear, so say it, a lot. Your au pair wants to feel appreciated for caring for your children. She may or may not want to really be a part of your family, but she does want to feel that she has made the right choice in being an au pair for a year. A simple "thank you" validates this choice and keeps her happy.

If you stick with the program long enough, you will find that your au pairs become a part of your family. Your extended family will reach around the world, and your holiday-card list will grow with many international addresses. You will begin to see that spending a year as an au pair, as *your* au pair, truly shapes the lives of these young people. As I look at the fourteen young people we have hosted in our home, I am incredibly proud of their accomplishments, and it makes me feel great to know that we have helped them along the way.

Thank you, and good luck with your next au pair!

✱ Activities won't do?
✱ Role in discipline?
✱ time off / vacation / holiday

APPENDICES

APPENDIX A

Telephone Interview Cheat Sheet
These questions do not have to be asked in the first call, but over the course of several phone calls—definitely before you match—you should get to all these points.

SLOWLY.

Hi, my name is _____ and I am looking for an au pair. Have you found a family yet? Is this a good time to talk?

Let me tell you a bit about us, and then you can tell me about you. OK?

We live in _____. We have ____ children. They are ages ____. I work as a(n) _____. My spouse works as a(n) _____. Our au pair is responsible for [describe duties and working hours of au pair].

So, why do you want to come to America to be an au pair?

Tell me about your family. Do you have brothers and sisters? How do they feel about your decision to be an au pair?

Do you know anyone who has been an au pair before?

Do you have pets? Do you like pets?

What do you like to do in your spare time?

Are you going to school right now? Are you working? Tell me about what you are doing right now. Describe your daily routine.

Have you ever lived away from home before? How have you dealt with being homesick?

Have you ever traveled to America before? Anywhere else? With whom? For how long?

How long have you been driving? Have you ever had a car accident? Are you comfortable driving in the snow? Do you drive a standard or automatic? How often do you drive? What kind of roads do you drive on? What side of the road do you drive on? Do you have experience driving on highways? What sort of driving do you have to do to get a driver's license in your home country?

Tell me about your experiences watching children.

What do you want to do while you are in the United States? Where would you like to travel? What things would you like to see?

Do you have a boyfriend or girlfriend? How does he or she feel about you coming to America to be an au pair?

What do you plan to do after your au pair year is over?

Do you eat a special diet? Will you seek out certain foods when you are in America?

APPENDIX B

Au Pair Glossary of Terms

au pair: A person, usually a young foreign visitor, employed "on par" to take care of children in exchange for room and board.

cluster: Geographic region managed by a local coordinator. Each local coordinator manages fifty to seventy-five au pair families.

cluster activity: Monthly or bimonthly activities organized by the local coordinator for the au pairs in a cluster.

educational requirement: The Department of State requirement that all au pairs complete sixty hours of college coursework during their year as an au pair.

extension: Instituted in 2005, the Department of State allowance that extends the J-1 visa for an additional six, nine, or twelve months.

floater pool: A group of all au pairs who have not had a successful match and in-country au pairs. All families looking for an au pair may look to find a new au pair from the floater pool.

host family: The family that hires an au pair.

in-country au pair: An au pair seeking to extend her J-1 visa but change host families. In-country au pairs are in the floater pool. If in rematch, a host family may wish to look at an in-country au pair from the floater pool.

J-1: Type of visa, issued by the Department of State, that allows an au pair to work in the United States.

local coordinator: The agency representative in charge of marketing the au pair program to prospective families and providing support to families and au pairs in his or her cluster. The local coordinator arranges cluster events.

match: When a host family offers the position of au pair to a foreign young person and the au pair accepts.

match fee: The fee paid to the sponsoring organization or au pair agency when a match is made and an au pair is hired by a host family.

rematch: If a match is not successful, a host family may rematch, firing their current au pair and hiring another au pair. An au pair may also request a rematch and will be given two weeks to find a new family.

sponsoring organization: The State Department term for an au pair agency. Twelve sponsoring organizations are sanctioned by the State Department to arrange au pair matches.

APPENDIX C: Au Pair Manual

WELCOME, AU PAIR!

Everything You Ever Wanted to Know about Your Host Family

Home Address (YOUR address)
Your address here

Important Phone Numbers
Home:
Your Cell:
Kid's Cell:
Mom's Cell:
Mom's Office:
Dad's Cell:
Dad's Office:
Au Pair Agency Coordinator:

Emergency Phone Numbers
911 for all emergencies – fire, ambulance, police
Town Police Department
800-962-1253 for Poison Control Center

CHILDCARE RESPONSIBILITIES

SCHOOL YEAR SCHEDULE

Care for children during the day M–F, 6:45 a.m.–8:00 a.m., and then from 3:00 p.m.–~6:00 p.m.

Every day, Will leaves for school at 7:30 a.m. and Hank leaves for school at 8:00 a.m. You should make breakfast for the boys and pack Hank's lunch each day. Will buys his lunch at school.

After the boys leave for school, you should take about forty-five minutes to one hour to do the boys' laundry, to clean up their rooms, to clean up the kitchen from breakfast, straighten up rooms, and put away toys, etc. The playroom in the basement should be vacuumed twice per week.

Each afternoon, the boys get home at about 3:15 p.m. After school, you should make sure that each boy gets a snack. After the snack, the boys should do their homework. While they are doing their homework, you should clean up Hank's lunch bags and remove notices from their backpacks. Around 5:30 or 6:00 p.m., Nancy usually gets home from work. Here is a sample schedule:

Mon – Fri: 6:45 a.m.: Begin work
7:00 a.m.: Mark and Nancy leave for work
7:00 a.m.–8:00 a.m.: Get the kids ready for school
7:30 a.m.: Will leaves for school
8:00 a.m.: Hank leaves for school
8:00 a.m.–9:00 a.m.: Household chores
9:00 a.m.–3:00 p.m.: Your free time

3:15 p.m.: Boys get home from school
3:15 p.m.– ~6:00 p.m.: Lessons, homework,
snack, playdates, have fun!

Hank's Lunch

Packed in his lunchbox
- ✓ One drinkable yogurt (in a tube) from the freezer
- ✓ Salty snack in a snack bag or in a plastic container with a top: Cheez-Its, Wheat Thins, Triscuits, pretzels, or Ritz crackers
- ✓ Cookies in a plastic container with a top

No candy or nuts in Hank's lunch!

Homework

After school each day, Will and Hank must do their homework. If possible, they must do their homework before any playdates. If a playdate is at our house, try to have them all do at least some of their homework together.

Ask both boys what they have for homework and check their planners to see what they have written down. In addition to daily homework, please ask each boy about upcoming tests and projects. If they have a test, please make sure you quiz them or ask what they need to do to get ready. If they have a project due, please help them to plan to get the work done in advance. The boys will often forget about homework or projects or practicing their instruments, so you will really need to check and double-check with them on what they have to get done. This is an important priority.

Please check Hank's homework when he is done and point out any errors. Have him re-check his work, and help make corrections.

In addition to homework, Will should practice the trumpet and the piano every day.

Playdates

Hank can have playdates on days when he does not have other activities. Playdates should last until 5 p.m. Make sure to arrange with the other parent who will do the pickup or the drop-off at the end of the playdate.

It is important to arrange pickup times for playdates when they begin. Do not let other mothers drop off kids with no pickup time. Also, the playdates should happen sometimes at our house and sometimes at the other children's houses. We do not want other moms to take advantage of you!

Hank's Frequent Playdates:

List contact info of your kids' friends and their parents or babysitters.

Activities

The family calendar is kept on the refrigerator. Please mark all your plans on the calendar, especially time for your classes, Au Pair Agency events, time off, and trips. Try to do this as early as you can so we can plan around the times you will be busy.

There are several weekday nights per month that Nancy and Mark have meetings or that they may be late. Please see the calendar for those nights that we will need you to work later. There are also some mornings when Nancy has to leave early – at 6:20 a.m.

During the school year, we will ask you to babysit about three or four weekend nights per month, but we will also give you at least one full weekend per month off. I will always put these dates on the calendar. We expect that the average work-week will be about forty-five hours.

We tend to go out early. You can always make plans to go out after we get home from an evening out.

SUMMER SCHEDULE
School ends in late June. During the summer months, your hours will increase because you are responsible for the boys during the days, but there are many fewer nighttime hours. The boys will do many activities during the summer—such as day camps and scout trips—which we will organize as the time gets closer.

Please encourage the children to read a lot during the summer.

OTHER RESPONSIBILITIES

Each morning, I ask that you do a few household chores:

✓ Make the boys' beds and pick up their rooms. Generally, I want the boys to clean their own rooms, but this doesn't always happen. You should remind the boys that they need to pick up their rooms, and help them to do so. Every day, please make sure that the beds are made, toys and clothes are picked up, and the bookshelves are kept neat so the boys can find and pull out books. Change/wash their sheets twice per month or more frequently if needed.

✓ Keep the rooms where the boys play neat, helping Will and Hank pick up. Please vacuum when needed (for example, the basement should be vacuumed twice per week). The boys tend to leave shoes, coats, socks, and other things around the house. Please direct them to put their things back where they belong and make sure that the house is kept neat. Toys should be kept either in the basement or in their rooms—not on the first floor.

✓ Keep the basement neat, and keep the toys organized. Please vacuum twice per week or as needed.

✓ Keep the kitchen neat—load and/or unload the dishwasher, wipe down countertops, put food away, and wash dishes and/or pots and pans. Clean up after kitchen projects with the kids. When you run the dishwasher, be sure to add dishwasher soap. The dishwasher soap is located under the kitchen sink.

✓ Make sure that the kids brush their teeth after breakfast and before school. Ask Hank if he has his retainer in his mouth when he is on the way to school.

✓ Please do their laundry twice per week or as needed, and please make sure you do your laundry and the children's laundry during the week. We do our laundry on the weekends. To keep the boys' clothes separate, you should do Hank's laundry one day and Will's laundry the next day. Please fold their laundry and put it away in their drawers. If any clothes need to be repaired, please leave them on the dryer in the laundry room. Do not put clothes away that are folded "inside out." Please make sure that all clothes are folded "right-side out."

Food Rules

Hank is a very picky eater. Right now, he eats the following foods:

- ✓ Drinkable yogurt
- ✓ Homemade waffles
- ✓ Coffee cakes
- ✓ Pretzels
- ✓ Peanuts
- ✓ Pistachios
- ✓ Wheat crackers
- ✓ Cheese crackers
- ✓ Noodles with butter
- ✓ Frozen corn with butter
- ✓ Cheerios cereal
- ✓ Hash brown potatoes
- ✓ Rice with butter
- ✓ Soft-boiled eggs (sometimes)
- ✓ Toast with butter
- ✓ French fries
- ✓ Chicken nuggets
- ✓ Baked potatoes

Please always try to introduce new foods to him, especially healthy foods. Maybe someday he will try something new!

The following foods should only given to Hank only in moderation:

- ✓ Potato chips
- ✓ Cheez-Its
- ✓ Popcorn

The following foods are "treats"—no more than one per day:

- ✓ Ice cream
- ✓ Chocolate
- ✓ Candy
- ✓ Cookies/brownies

The boys may not eat in the sitting room. Whenever possible, meals should be eaten at the kitchen table or (in the summer) on the porch table. The boys may take food to the basement but must clean up all their garbage. The boys are not allowed to bring food upstairs.

Please let us know if you would like anything special from the grocery store.

Activities to Do with the Boys

- ✓ Play outside (we like the kids to be as active as possible)
- ✓ Play board games
- ✓ Play pool
- ✓ Walk the dog

✓ Play computer games/video games (but don't let the boys do this too much)
✓ Go to the park/take the dog to the dog park
✓ Bake/cook
✓ Go to the library
✓ Read books
✓ Ride bikes, scooters. Helmets must be worn when riding bikes.

Supplies for arts and crafts are kept in the cabinet underneath the small sink in the pantry, next to the kitchen. If you need anything or if we run out of supplies, just ask. We will be happy to give you money for things.

You may watch movies with the boys on special occasions—on demand or on DVD. Please be aware of the rating of a movie that the children want to watch. There is a system in the United States that assigns a rating to a movie. The ratings are G, PG, PG-13, and R. The boys are allowed to watch any movie that is G, PG, or PG-13. They are not allowed to watch R-rated movies.

Bedtime Routine

The boys go to bed around 8:30 p.m. On most nights, we will put the boys to bed. There are some occasions when you will need to put the boys to bed. When you do, take the boys upstairs and make sure that they brush their teeth, go to the bathroom, wash their hands and faces, and change into their pajamas. Once in their beds, they should read for at least thirty minutes. It is OK for the boys to read with book lights after you say good night. It is OK to turn the radio on with a low volume.

If we are home, we will take care of the bedtime routine. If we are out and you are babysitting, you will need to do this.

FIRST AID

There is a first-aid kit with Band-Aids in the cabinet above the toilet in the downstairs bathroom.

TELEPHONE

We will give you a cell phone (phone # XXX-XXX-XXXX). Please keep this phone with you at all times. You are allowed to make calls within the United States with this phone. Call us or text us at any time wherever we are if there is a problem. Common numbers (for us, for our family, etc.) are programmed into the phone already. You also have voice mail on this phone. To access your voice mail, press and hold the 1 key. You should not have to enter a password. Press 1 to hear your messages. If you want to delete your message, press 7 when it is done.

The phone plan allows for 400 text messages per month and 1000 minutes. Minutes are used regardless of whether you call or someone else calls you.

DISCIPLINE

You are in charge. If the children misbehave, you should discipline them. The first thing to do is to tell them that you have noticed that they are misbehaving and that they should change their behavior. If they choose not to change their behavior, or if they have done something serious, you should send them to their room for fifteen or thirty minutes.

Sometimes when they fight, they'll want to call us on our cell phones. Please have the boys try to resolve the issue themselves. If it is very difficult, it's OK for them to call us, but only as a last resort.

If the boys are fighting, the best thing to do is to separate them.

Please tell us when the boys have misbehaved. It is important that they know that we are all communicating about their behavior and our expectations of them.

HOUSE RULES

1. No food upstairs, ever.

2. No candles or flames of any kind, anywhere.

3. No TV after school Monday–Thursday.

4. Read every day.

CONTACT INFORMATION

Mom at Work

Name of Company
Address of Company
City, State, Zip
Telephone Number
E-mail Address

Neighbors/Friends

[List three or four people including contact information whom your au pair could call for help if she can't contact you.]

Family

[List all family members. I list these so my au pair can recognize names when I say them and understand where our families live.]

SCHOOL INFORMATION

Child's School

Name of School
Telephone Number of School
Child's Grade and Teacher
School starts promptly at 8:00 a.m.

Child's School

Name of School
Telephone Number of School
Child's Grade and Teacher
School starts promptly at 8:20 a.m.

HOUSE INFORMATION

Mail: Delivered to our house every day around 10 a.m. The dog cannot be outside when the mailman comes, or he will not deliver the mail.

Garbage Pickup: Tuesday mornings and Friday mornings. The dog must be inside when the garbage men come to pick up the garbage.

Recycling: (Newspapers only in bags AND cans and bottles in bin) 1st and 3rd Wednesday of every month.

Oil Delivery: 3–4 times per year, a big truck comes and delivers oil for our heat. If the car is in the driveway, it may need to be moved.

Telephone: Please use a calling card for long-distance phone calls. Local calls are fine.

Guests: No problem. Just let us know if you plan to have guests over.

Alarm: If the alarm sounds, the alarm company—Home Protection Company—will call. They will ask you the "secret" code word, which is XXYY. If you would like them to send the police, they will do so.

Lawn Service: In the spring and summer, the lawn service comes once a week.

Cleaning Lady: Our cleaning person comes every other week on Wednesdays. She comes at about 7:30 and stays until about noon.

Repairs: If there is something in the house that needs to be repaired, please let us know.

MEDICAL INFORMATION

The boys have no real health concerns.

Will has an allergy to shellfish. If for some reason he thinks that he has been exposed, he will get a scratchy throat. For this, he should get Benadryl right away. The Benadryl is kept in the kitchen drawer with the vitamins. The first-aid kit and Band-Aids are kept in the medicine cabinet in the first-floor bathroom. If the boys are sick, they will stay home from school, and you will need to stay with them.

Will and Hank's Doctor

Dr. Jones and Dr. Smith
Telephone Number
Address
City, State, Zip
Driving Instructions

General Doctor (if you need to see a doctor)

Dr. Jones and Dr. Smith
Telephone Number
Address
City, State, Zip

The nearest hospital is Mountainview Hospital on Main Avenue. It is about a five-minute drive. The children's doctors go to St. Barnabas Medical Center, about a twenty-minute drive. If at all possible, go to St. Barnabas.

Driving instructions:

DOG'S INFORMATION

[Name of dog] is a X-year-old [breed of dog]. She weighs about [XX pounds.

Veterinarian

Dr. Cats
Cats and Dogs Animal Hospital
Telephone Number
Address
City, State, Zip
Driving Instructions

Kennel
Cats and Dogs Animal Hotel
Telephone Number
Address
City, State, Zip
Driving Instructions

When you leave the house, please put the dog in her crate.

CAR INFORMATION

Car #1: License Plate #
Car #2: License Plate #

You must have your International Driving Permit with you whenever you are driving. The registration and insurance card are kept in the glove compartment. If you are ever "pulled over" by a policeman, you will need to show your license, the registration, and the insurance card.

Always be careful where you park the car. You must never park in front of a fire hydrant or against a curb that is painted yellow. If you park in a parking place that has a meter, you must put money in the meter. You do NOT have to put money in the meter if it is Sunday or after 5 p.m. When you go to the gym, you will be responsible for the parking meter.

Please keep the cars clean. Ask the children to take out all items they bring into the car to keep it tidy. Please keep gas in the cars. On the key chain is a Speedpass (small black plastic), which allows you to purchase gas at many Mobil and Exxon stations in the area. Ask if they have Speedpass before they pump. All gas stations in New Jersey are "full serve," which means that someone will pump the gas for you. You give them the Speedpass, and they will pump and give you a receipt. Please buy "regular unleaded" gas.

Some highways require tolls. In all our cars, we have an automatic payment system called EZPass, which is located on the windshield. If you are driving on the highway and come to a toll booth, proceed through the ones with the purple signs overhead that say EZPass. You will be able to drive right through after you see a green light indicating it has "read" our EZPass.

If anything happens to the car, please let us know immediately. If anything seems wrong with the car, please let us know immediately.

Do not let anyone else drive our cars. Do not ever drink and drive. Please call for a taxi or call us to come get you if you have a problem or need a ride.

YOUR TIME OFF

Please let us know in advance if you would like time off, and mark the calendar. You have two weeks of vacation—both will be paid. We will give you one full weekend off per month, especially if you have a trip planned. Please take advantage of all the great destinations that are just a train ride or a short drive away! We will always pay you for the whole week, even if we are away.

You are welcome to spend time in any room in the house. The TV in the basement can show DVDs and videos. Will can show you how to use it. Please feel free to rent DVDs or videos at any time.

We have a membership for our au pair at the YMCA. The cost is $50/month, and we pay for $30/month of the fee. If you are interested in using this facility to exercise, we will continue the membership and deduct $5 from your pay every week. Mark will show you the YMCA.

Your educational requirement: There are several colleges in our area to look into:

✓ [LIST LOCAL COLLEGES – Provide Web site links]

OTHER

You are responsible for cleaning your room and your bathroom. Cleaning supplies can be found in the closet next to the washer and the dryer or under the sink in the kitchen. Analea, our cleaning lady, does not clean your room or your bathroom. You must clean the toilet with cleaner and the scrub brush provided. Frequently wipe down the tiles in the shower. Please let us know if you need anything. If anything needs repaired, please let us know as soon as possible.

You are required to attend Au Pair Agency events. Please write them on the calendar as soon as you know when they will take place.

If you need to mail anything, the post office is at [ADDRESS].

LEAVING KIDS HOME ALONE

You may leave Will home alone. You can leave Hank home alone for up to ten minutes. Do not leave him alone for longer than that.

COMPUTERS

There are three computers in the house: two computers down-stairs and a laptop. You are welcome to use any of the computers. There is wireless Internet access also.

FINANCIAL ISSUES

We will pay you $XXX each week on Fridays. We will give you money when needed for activities with the boys. We will help you to open a bank account at our bank. If you establish an account here, we will arrange a direct deposit into your account each Friday. Your account will come with a Visa debit card, and you will be mailed monthly statements.

You are responsible for paying U.S. income tax on your pay. This will be about $XXX for the year. If you would like me to withhold money each month, please let me know.

CPSIA information can be obtained at www.ICGtesting.com
Printed in the USA
BVOW05s0533210116

433740BV00031BC/361/P